Self-Driving Cars and AI

How Autonomous Vehicles are Changing Transportation A Guide to AI in Mobility, Machine Learning, and Automotive Innovation

Greyson Chesterfield

COPYRIGHT

DISCLAIMER

The information provided in this book is for general informational purposes only. All content in this book reflects the author's views and is based on their research, knowledge, and experiences. The author and publisher make no representations or warranties of any kind concerning the completeness, accuracy, reliability, suitability, or availability of the information contained herein.

This book is not intended to be a substitute for professional advice, diagnosis, or treatment. Readers should seek professional advice for any specific concerns or conditions. The author and publisher disclaim any liability or responsibility for any direct, indirect, incidental, or consequential loss or damage arising from the use of the information contained in this book.

Chapter 9: AI and Robotics in Vehicle Manufacturing.. 141

Introduction to Autonomous Vehicles and AI

Introduction to Autonomous Vehicles (AVs)

Autonomous vehicles (AVs), often called self-driving cars, represent a groundbreaking shift in the transportation industry, blending cutting-edge technologies with the aim of transforming the way we navigate the world. AVs are designed to operate with minimal human intervention, using a combination of sensors, cameras, radar, and advanced algorithms to understand their environment, make decisions, and move accordingly. The ultimate goal is to create a safer, more efficient, and sustainable mode of transportation. Over the years, AV technology has evolved from an academic dream into a real-world application that is gradually becoming more integrated into industries such as logistics, healthcare, and public transportation.

The History of AI in Transportation

The journey of AI in transportation dates back decades, starting with early attempts at creating self-driving cars in the 1950s. However, the true integration of AI in transportation began in earnest in the 1980s and 1990s with breakthroughs in machine learning and computer vision, which provided the computational power necessary for AVs to operate safely. Early experiments were mostly conducted by academic institutions, but by the early 2000s, large tech companies like Google, Tesla, and Uber began to spearhead the commercialization of AVs. This period saw significant advancements in machine learning algorithms, which enabled vehicles to process and interpret vast amounts of real-time data, paving the way for the sophisticated self-driving systems we have today. Throughout this history, AI has played a critical role in enabling AVs to perceive the world, make decisions, and execute driving tasks.

Understanding the Technology Behind Autonomous Vehicles

At the heart of autonomous vehicles is a complex network of technologies that work in harmony to ensure the vehicle can navigate its environment safely and efficiently. The most critical components of this technology include:

1. **Sensors and Perception**
   Autonomous vehicles rely on a range of sensors, such as radar, lidar (light detection and ranging), ultrasonic sensors, and cameras, to gather information about their environment. These sensors create a detailed map of the surroundings, detecting obstacles, lane markings, traffic signals, pedestrians, and other vehicles. Sensor fusion algorithms combine data from multiple sensors to create an accurate, real-time picture of the vehicle's environment, allowing it to make informed decisions.

2. **Machine Learning and AI Algorithms**
   The core functionality of an autonomous vehicle is powered by machine learning algorithms. These algorithms use vast amounts

of data collected from both real-world driving and simulation environments to improve the vehicle's ability to recognize patterns, make decisions, and predict outcomes. The vehicle's AI system is trained on a variety of driving scenarios, enabling it to understand traffic laws, road conditions, and pedestrian behaviors. Reinforcement learning, supervised learning, and unsupervised learning play key roles in how AVs develop their decision-making processes, allowing them to learn from both successful and failed driving experiences.

3. **Mapping and Localization**
   Self-driving cars need highly accurate maps of the roads they travel on. These maps include details like lane markings, intersections, traffic signals, and the positions of curbs and other objects. High-definition maps are used in combination with real-time sensor data to help the vehicle understand its exact location on the road, even in complex environments. Localization is the process of determining the vehicle's precise position in relation to the map, ensuring it stays on the correct path and avoids potential hazards.

4. **Vehicle Control and Decision-Making**

   Once the sensors and AI systems understand the environment, they must decide how to act. This involves determining the best course of action, whether it's braking, accelerating, steering, or signaling. The vehicle's AI must make decisions in real-time while considering the safety and efficiency of its actions. This decision-making process relies heavily on deep learning models that predict the best outcomes based on past experiences, driving rules, and the current traffic scenario.

Real-World Applications of Autonomous Vehicles

1. Logistics and Delivery

Autonomous vehicles are revolutionizing logistics by offering more efficient, reliable, and cost-effective solutions for transporting goods. Companies like Amazon, Waymo, and TuSimple are investing heavily in self-driving trucks and delivery vans to streamline the delivery process. These vehicles are capable of driving long distances without the need for human drivers, reducing operational costs and minimizing delivery times. In addition, autonomous delivery robots, such as those developed by Starship Technologies, are being used for last-mile deliveries, providing an eco-friendly solution for short-distance package transportation.

2. Ride-Hailing and Passenger Transportation

Ride-hailing companies such as Uber and Lyft are exploring the use of autonomous vehicles to reduce costs and improve the efficiency of their services. Self-driving cars can help cut down on human driver expenses while enhancing passenger experience by providing more reliable, on-demand transportation options. Additionally, autonomous vehicles could increase access to transportation for people with disabilities, elderly passengers, or those in underserved areas.

3. Healthcare and Medical Transport

In healthcare, autonomous vehicles have the potential to play a crucial role in improving medical transportation. Self-driving cars can be used for non-emergency medical transport, such as taking patients to regular doctor's appointments or transporting medical supplies. They can also be used for emergency medical services, offering faster response times by reducing the need for human drivers. Furthermore, AVs can be integrated with healthcare systems to improve the efficiency of hospital logistics, including the transportation of drugs, lab samples, and medical equipment.

4. Public Transportation

Public transit is another area where AVs are making strides. Self-driving buses, trams, and shuttles are being tested in cities around the world as part of smart city initiatives. These autonomous vehicles can help reduce congestion and increase the availability of transportation in areas that have historically had limited transit options. Self-driving buses, in particular, are seen as a way to provide cost-effective solutions for mass transit, particularly in less dense urban areas or on fixed routes.

5. Autonomous Vehicles in Agriculture

AI-powered autonomous vehicles are also being applied to the agricultural sector, helping farmers increase efficiency and reduce labor costs. Self-driving tractors, harvesters, and other farming machinery are already in use to autonomously plow fields, plant crops, and even harvest produce. These vehicles are equipped with sensors and AI algorithms that allow them to operate efficiently and make real-time decisions based on environmental conditions, ensuring optimal crop yield while reducing waste.

The Role of Machine Learning and AI in Autonomous Vehicle Development

1. Machine Learning in Perception and Object Recognition

Machine learning plays a pivotal role in how autonomous vehicles interpret the world around them. The first task is to recognize and classify objects, whether they are pedestrians, cyclists, other vehicles, road signs, or obstacles. Convolutional neural networks (CNNs) are commonly used in image recognition tasks to process data from cameras and identify objects. The more diverse and accurate the training data, the better the machine learning model can perform in real-world scenarios.

2. Reinforcement Learning in Decision Making

Reinforcement learning (RL) is a form of machine

learning where the AV learns by interacting with its environment and receiving feedback. RL enables autonomous vehicles to learn optimal decision-making strategies through trial and error. This is particularly useful for tasks like lane merging, yielding at intersections, and navigating through complex traffic situations. By receiving rewards for successful outcomes and penalties for mistakes, RL allows AVs to improve their behavior over time.

3. Deep Learning for Advanced Perception

Deep learning techniques, such as deep reinforcement learning (DRL), are employed to tackle more complex tasks in autonomous vehicles. These models help AVs understand complicated scenarios, such as recognizing different types of pedestrians (e.g., adults vs. children) or determining the intentions of other drivers. For example, by analyzing vast amounts of data from traffic cameras, deep learning algorithms can discern when a pedestrian is likely to cross the road or when another vehicle is signaling to change lanes.

4. AI for Predictive Analytics and Risk Assessment

AI-powered predictive analytics can help autonomous vehicles assess risks and make proactive decisions.

By analyzing historical data and real-time sensor inputs, AI models can predict future events and mitigate potential accidents. This includes predicting the behavior of other drivers, anticipating road conditions (e.g., icy roads), and calculating the safest routes. Predictive models can improve safety and efficiency by allowing AVs to anticipate and react to scenarios before they unfold.

Conclusion

The development of autonomous vehicles powered by artificial intelligence is revolutionizing transportation. As the technology continues to advance, we are witnessing profound changes in how goods and people are transported, leading to more efficient, safer, and sustainable systems. Machine learning and AI are at the core of these advancements, helping AVs perceive their environment, make decisions, and optimize their performance. As the world continues to embrace AI in transportation, industries such as logistics, healthcare, and public transport will see further transformations, pushing the boundaries of what autonomous vehicles can achieve. With the right blend of technology, policy, and innovation, the road ahead for autonomous vehicles is one full of promise and potential.

Chapter 2: The Fundamentals of Self-Driving Cars

Introduction to Self-Driving Cars

Self-driving cars, also known as autonomous vehicles (AVs), represent a significant leap forward in automotive technology. These cars are designed to navigate the world with minimal human input, relying on complex systems that allow them to perceive their environment, make decisions, and control their movements. While the concept of autonomous driving has existed for decades, it has only been in the last two decades that we have witnessed remarkable advancements in the field. By combining cutting-edge hardware such as sensors and cameras with sophisticated software algorithms driven by artificial intelligence (AI), self-driving cars are now capable of performing driving tasks traditionally handled by humans.

In this chapter, we will break down the fundamental components that make up an autonomous vehicle, how these components work together to enable self-driving, and the critical role data collection and processing play in the operation of these vehicles.

1. Key Components of Self-Driving Cars: Sensors, Cameras, Radar, and LIDAR

1.1 Sensors: The Eyes of the Car

Sensors are at the core of how a self-driving car perceives the world. These devices gather environmental data, which is then processed and analyzed by the vehicle's onboard computer systems to make decisions. There are several types of sensors used in autonomous vehicles, each contributing unique capabilities.

1. **Radar (Radio Detection and Ranging):** Radar is one of the primary sensors in autonomous vehicles. It uses electromagnetic waves to detect objects and measure their

distance, speed, and direction. Radar excels in detecting objects in low visibility conditions, such as rain, fog, or darkness. This makes it an essential tool for AVs when navigating in unpredictable weather conditions. Radar sensors typically operate at longer ranges than cameras, allowing self-driving cars to "see" objects from a distance, even when they are outside the view of other sensors.

- ○ **Application in Autonomous Vehicles:** Radar is particularly valuable for detecting large obstacles, like other vehicles or trucks, and for adaptive cruise control, which maintains a safe distance from the vehicle ahead.

2. **Cameras:**
Cameras provide high-resolution visual data, allowing self-driving cars to "see" much like humans do. They are vital for recognizing objects, traffic signs, road markings, pedestrians, and other dynamic elements of the road. Cameras are crucial for visual tasks like lane detection and traffic signal recognition. They are integrated with computer vision

algorithms, which allow the vehicle to interpret the image data and understand the environment.

- o **Application in Autonomous Vehicles:** Cameras are used to help self-driving cars stay within lanes, identify road signs and traffic lights, and detect obstacles such as pedestrians or cyclists.

3. **LIDAR (Light Detection and Ranging):** LIDAR uses laser light to measure distances and create a detailed 3D map of the environment. LIDAR sensors emit rapid laser pulses and measure the time it takes for the pulses to bounce back from objects. This technology produces highly accurate data and is capable of generating high-definition 3D maps in real-time, providing the vehicle with a detailed understanding of its surroundings. LIDAR is crucial for precise localization and obstacle detection, especially in environments where other sensors, like cameras, might struggle.

- o **Application in Autonomous Vehicles:** LIDAR provides a detailed, 360-degree view of the environment, enabling AVs to map their surroundings in real-time, detect obstacles, and navigate safely through complex environments like city streets or parking lots.

4. **Ultrasonic Sensors:**
   Ultrasonic sensors emit sound waves and measure the time it takes for them to return after hitting an object. These sensors are typically used for close-range detection and are often employed for tasks like parking, low-speed maneuvering, and detecting objects in the vehicle's immediate surroundings.

   o **Application in Autonomous Vehicles:**
   Ultrasonic sensors are used for parking assist, detecting curbs, and helping AVs navigate tight spaces where precision is crucial.

2. The Importance of Data Collection and Processing

Self-driving cars generate vast amounts of data every second as they navigate the road. The data collected by sensors is not only critical for immediate driving decisions but also for improving the car's performance over time through machine learning.

2.1 Real-Time Data Processing:

Real-time data processing is essential for ensuring that autonomous vehicles can make fast, accurate decisions while driving. When a self-driving car moves through its environment, it collects and processes data from sensors at rapid intervals. This real-time data allows the car to interpret the environment and make instantaneous decisions, such as braking to avoid a pedestrian or steering to avoid an obstacle.

- **Example:** A self-driving car might detect a pedestrian crossing the street using its cameras and LIDAR. In less than a fraction of a second, the car must decide whether to brake or accelerate, using the data from its sensors and the real-time environment.

2.2 Data Fusion and Sensor Integration:

To ensure accurate decision-making, the data from various sensors must be integrated or "fused" into a cohesive understanding of the environment. This process is known as sensor fusion, and it involves combining data from radar, LIDAR, cameras, and ultrasonic sensors to create a unified map of the car's surroundings. Sensor fusion allows the vehicle to overcome the limitations of individual sensors by filling in the gaps.

- **Example:** Radar might detect an object in the distance, while a camera might identify it as a red light. LIDAR helps pinpoint the exact location of the light in three-dimensional space. Together, these sensors give the car a complete picture of its environment.

2.3 Machine Learning and Data Training:

The data collected from real-world driving scenarios is used to train machine learning algorithms, enabling autonomous vehicles to improve their ability to recognize patterns and make decisions. Over time, the system learns from both successes and mistakes, making it more reliable. The more data an AV collects, the better it becomes at predicting various driving scenarios and improving its safety and efficiency.

- **Example:** A machine learning algorithm might be trained to recognize different types of pedestrians. The system "learns" by processing thousands of images of people on the road, teaching it to detect a range of pedestrian behaviors and predict when they might cross the street.

3. How Self-Driving Cars "See" and Interpret Their Surroundings

Self-driving cars rely on an array of sensors and artificial intelligence to understand the environment around them. While these vehicles don't "see" in the same way that humans do, the combination of sensors, computer vision, and AI gives them the ability to perceive their surroundings and make informed decisions.

3.1 The Role of Computer Vision:

Computer vision is a subset of AI that allows computers to interpret and understand visual data. In self-driving cars, computer vision algorithms process camera inputs to detect and identify objects, such as pedestrians, road signs, and traffic signals. These algorithms use techniques such as image recognition and object detection to analyze the data and "understand" the environment.

- **Example:** When a self-driving car approaches an intersection, its cameras use computer vision to identify the traffic lights and determine whether they are red, green, or yellow.

3.2 Object Detection and Classification:

Object detection is the process by which a self-driving car identifies and classifies objects in its environment. The car uses AI algorithms to recognize different objects, such as other vehicles, pedestrians, or road hazards. This classification allows the vehicle to prioritize its actions and react accordingly.

- **Example:** The vehicle's system might classify an object as a pedestrian, cyclist, or stationary object, and decide whether to slow down, stop, or navigate around it.

3.3 Semantic Segmentation:

Semantic segmentation is a technique used in self-driving cars to label each pixel of an image with a corresponding category, such as road, sidewalk, car, or pedestrian. This granular understanding of the environment helps the vehicle make decisions based on a more detailed map of its surroundings.

- **Example:** By segmenting an image of a road, the AV can separate the road from the sidewalk, allowing it to navigate within the proper lane and avoid pedestrians on the sidewalk.

4. Step-by-Step Breakdown of a Self-Driving Car's Architecture

4.1 The Overall System Architecture:

At a high level, the self-driving car's architecture is divided into several key systems: perception, planning, decision-making, and control. These systems work in tandem to enable the car to navigate the world autonomously.

1. **Perception:**

   This system is responsible for gathering and processing data from sensors, such as cameras, LIDAR, radar, and ultrasonic sensors. It uses this data to build a detailed understanding of the vehicle's environment.

2. **Planning:**

   The planning system takes the data from the perception system and decides on a path for the vehicle to follow. This includes making high-level decisions such as route planning and lower-level decisions like turning or changing lanes.

3. **Decision-Making:**

   The decision-making system is responsible for determining the car's next move. It must decide how to react to dynamic situations, such as the behavior of other drivers, pedestrians, or unexpected road conditions.

4. **Control:**

   The control system ensures that the vehicle

executes the planned trajectory. It controls the car's acceleration, braking, and steering, ensuring it stays within its lane, avoids obstacles, and reaches its destination safely.

4.2 Step-by-Step Process:

The architecture of an autonomous vehicle can be broken down into the following steps:

1. **Perception Layer:**
   Sensors gather data and create a 3D map of the environment.

2. **Localization Layer:**
   Using GPS and high-definition maps, the vehicle determines its precise location within the environment.

3. **Planning Layer:**
   The planning system processes the data and decides on the vehicle's trajectory.

4. **Control Layer:**
   The control system executes the planned trajectory and ensures the vehicle moves safely along the path.

Conclusion

Self-driving cars are a remarkable achievement of modern technology, combining multiple sensors, data processing techniques, and advanced AI algorithms to create a vehicle capable of navigating complex environments. By understanding how these cars "see" and interpret their surroundings, we can appreciate the intricate systems at work behind every autonomous drive. The architecture of self-driving cars, with its sophisticated perception, planning, and control systems, continues to evolve, and as these technologies improve, the future of autonomous driving becomes ever more promising.

Chapter 3: Understanding Machine Learning for Autonomous Vehicles

Introduction to Machine Learning and Deep Learning

In the world of autonomous vehicles (AVs), machine learning (ML) is the backbone that empowers these vehicles to learn from experience, adapt to different environments, and make decisions without human intervention. Machine learning allows AVs to analyze vast amounts of data, recognize patterns, and improve performance over time. Deep learning, a subset of machine learning, takes this concept further by leveraging complex neural networks to mimic the human brain's way of processing information, enabling AVs to perform tasks such as object detection, decision-making, and path planning.

3.1 What is Machine Learning?

Machine learning refers to the concept of using algorithms and statistical models to analyze data and make predictions or decisions based on that data, without explicitly programming the system for each decision. In the context of autonomous vehicles, machine learning enables the vehicle's systems to understand their environment, make real-time decisions, and improve their abilities over time based on new data.

For instance, a self-driving car needs to be able to recognize pedestrians, cyclists, road signs, and other vehicles on the road. Instead of hardcoding these rules, machine learning algorithms allow the car to learn these patterns from data, making it more adaptable to new and unseen situations.

- **Example in AVs:**
  The vehicle might encounter a new road sign it has never seen before. Through machine learning, the car can classify this new sign correctly by comparing its features to known patterns and make the appropriate decision, such as stopping at a traffic signal or yielding at a pedestrian crossing.

3.2 What is Deep Learning?

Deep learning is a more advanced form of machine learning that uses multi-layered neural networks to simulate the learning processes of the human brain. These deep neural networks are capable of learning from large amounts of unstructured data, making them highly effective in tasks like image recognition, speech processing, and natural language understanding. Deep learning has revolutionized the field of autonomous vehicles by enabling systems to make decisions based on high-dimensional data such as video feeds, sensor data, and lidar point clouds.

- **Example in AVs:**
  Deep learning is used in self-driving cars for object detection and classification. For example, using convolutional neural networks

(CNNs), a car can detect pedestrians, cyclists, or other vehicles by analyzing images from cameras in real-time. The car can then classify these objects and decide how to navigate around them.

Types of Machine Learning: Supervised, Unsupervised, and Reinforcement Learning

Machine learning can be classified into three main types: supervised learning, unsupervised learning, and reinforcement learning. Each of these learning paradigms has its unique strengths and applications in autonomous vehicle technology.

3.3 Supervised Learning

Supervised learning is the most common type of machine learning used in autonomous vehicles. In supervised learning, the model is trained on a labeled dataset, where the input data is paired with the correct output. The model learns to map inputs to outputs by minimizing errors through the training process. Once trained, the model can generalize to new, unseen data.

- **Example in AVs:**
  A supervised learning model might be trained on thousands of images of road signs, with each image labeled as a specific sign, such as "stop" or "yield." The model learns to classify road signs by associating pixel patterns with their respective labels. After training, the model can recognize road signs in real-world scenarios and make decisions based on the sign's meaning.

- **Real-World Use Case:**
  In AVs, supervised learning is commonly used for object detection and classification tasks. For example, cameras mounted on the car might capture images of pedestrians, and the supervised model would learn to classify them as people, distinguishing them from other objects like trees or lampposts.

3.4 Unsupervised Learning

Unsupervised learning, in contrast to supervised learning, involves training a model on data that does not have predefined labels. The goal of unsupervised learning is to identify patterns or structures in the data without prior knowledge of the outcomes. This type of learning is useful for tasks such as clustering, anomaly detection, and dimensionality reduction.

- **Example in AVs:**
  One application of unsupervised learning in AVs is in anomaly detection. By analyzing large amounts of sensor data from radar, lidar, and cameras, unsupervised learning can identify unusual patterns, such as objects that do not belong in the environment, which could be obstacles or hazards the vehicle needs to avoid.

- **Real-World Use Case:**
  Unsupervised learning is particularly useful in AVs when the car encounters situations it has not been explicitly trained for, such as recognizing new types of obstacles or road conditions. By clustering similar data points, the system can identify patterns that help the car adjust its behavior to new, unknown situations.

3.5 Reinforcement Learning

Reinforcement learning (RL) is a type of machine learning where an agent (in this case, the autonomous vehicle) learns by interacting with its environment and receiving feedback in the form of rewards or penalties. The agent explores different actions and learns the most optimal actions through trial and error. In AVs, reinforcement learning is particularly useful for tasks such as path planning, decision-making, and route optimization.

- **Example in AVs:**
  In reinforcement learning, a self-driving car might learn how to navigate a complex intersection by taking actions like stopping, accelerating, or turning. The car receives rewards for correct decisions (e.g., safely navigating through the intersection) and penalties for wrong decisions (e.g., causing a near-collision). Over time, the car refines its strategy to navigate intersections more efficiently and safely.

- **Real-World Use Case:**
  RL is used in AVs for complex decision-making tasks, such as determining when to change lanes, merge onto highways, or navigate in traffic. By learning from both successes and failures, RL allows AVs to optimize their driving strategies in diverse and dynamic environments.

Practical Use Cases of Machine Learning in Autonomous Vehicles

Machine learning plays a crucial role in enabling autonomous vehicles to navigate and interact with their environment. Below are some of the most common practical applications of machine learning in AVs:

3.6 Object Detection and Recognition

Object detection is one of the most critical tasks for autonomous vehicles. AVs must detect and classify various objects, such as pedestrians, cyclists, other vehicles, traffic signs, and road barriers, in real time. Machine learning algorithms, particularly deep learning models like convolutional neural networks (CNNs), are used for object detection and recognition tasks.

- **Example in AVs:**
  Using CNNs, AVs can recognize pedestrians in real-time by analyzing images from cameras. The vehicle can then decide to slow down or stop if a pedestrian is detected in the path. Object detection also enables the car to

distinguish between vehicles, cyclists, and pedestrians, allowing it to make safe driving decisions.

3.7 Path Planning and Decision-Making

Path planning involves calculating the optimal route that an autonomous vehicle should take to reach its destination while avoiding obstacles and obeying traffic laws. Reinforcement learning is often used in path planning, where the AV learns the best actions (e.g., turning, stopping, accelerating) by interacting with its environment.

- **Example in AVs:**
  In a real-world scenario, an autonomous vehicle might need to navigate through a busy city intersection. The vehicle must decide when to stop, yield, or proceed based on traffic lights, pedestrians, and other vehicles. Machine learning algorithms help the car make these decisions based on real-time sensor data.

3.8 Sensor Fusion

Sensor fusion is the process of combining data from multiple sensors, such as cameras, lidar, radar, and ultrasonic sensors, to create a unified and accurate representation of the environment. Machine learning algorithms play a crucial role in sensor fusion by analyzing data from different sources and integrating it into a comprehensive understanding of the surroundings.

- **Example in AVs:**
  A self-driving car might use lidar to detect the distance to nearby objects, radar to track moving objects like other vehicles, and cameras to recognize road signs. Machine learning algorithms combine this data to create a complete picture of the environment, allowing the car to make informed decisions.

Simple Project: Setting Up a Machine Learning Environment for AV Simulations

To understand the practical implementation of machine learning in autonomous vehicles, it is helpful to start with a simple project that sets up a machine learning environment for autonomous vehicle simulations. Below is a step-by-step guide to creating a basic simulation using a machine learning model for object detection.

3.9 Step 1: Install Required Tools and Libraries

To begin, you will need to install several tools and libraries necessary for working with machine learning and autonomous vehicle simulations:

- Python (latest version)

- TensorFlow or PyTorch (for machine learning)

- OpenCV (for computer vision)

- CARLA or LGSVL (for AV simulation environments)

- Jupyter Notebook (for easy testing and visualization)

3.10 Step 2: Load and Preprocess the Dataset

In this step, we will load a dataset of road images and labels (e.g., road signs, pedestrians). You can use an open-source dataset like the Berkeley DeepDrive dataset or create your own using simulated environments.

- Load images and corresponding labels (e.g., bounding boxes around objects).

- Preprocess the images by resizing, normalizing, and augmenting them.

3.11 Step 3: Train the Machine Learning Model

We will use a convolutional neural network (CNN) to train the model for object detection. Train the model using the preprocessed dataset, adjusting hyperparameters such as learning rate, batch size, and number of epochs.

- Example code snippet for training a CNN using TensorFlow:

python

Copy

```python
model = tf.keras.Sequential([
    tf.keras.layers.Conv2D(32, (3, 3), activation='relu', input_shape=(224, 224, 3)),
    tf.keras.layers.MaxPooling2D(2, 2),
    tf.keras.layers.Conv2D(64, (3, 3), activation='relu'),
    tf.keras.layers.MaxPooling2D(2, 2),
    tf.keras.layers.Flatten(),
    tf.keras.layers.Dense(128, activation='relu'),
```

```
    tf.keras.layers.Dense(num_classes,
activation='softmax')

])
```

3.12 Step 4: Test the Model in a Simulation Environment

Once the model is trained, you can test it in a simulated environment. Use a simulation platform like CARLA to simulate driving scenarios, such as detecting pedestrians or other vehicles.

- Load the trained model into the simulation environment.

- Monitor how the vehicle responds to detected objects in real-time.

Conclusion

Machine learning is at the heart of autonomous vehicles, enabling them to perceive their environment, make decisions, and improve their performance over time. By understanding the different types of machine learning (supervised, unsupervised, and reinforcement learning) and their practical applications, you can gain a deeper appreciation of how AVs function. The ability of machine learning to process large amounts of sensor data, detect objects, plan routes, and make decisions is essential to the development of autonomous vehicles. Through projects and simulations, we can gain hands-on experience with these concepts, preparing us for more advanced applications and real-world AV scenarios.

Chapter 4: Data Collection and Processing for Self-Driving Cars

Introduction to Data in Autonomous Vehicle Development

Data is the lifeblood of autonomous vehicle (AV) development. For self-driving cars to operate safely, efficiently, and autonomously, they must be able to sense and interpret the world around them in real-time. This requires an immense amount of data—both from sensors and external sources—that is processed, analyzed, and used to make driving decisions. In fact, the performance of autonomous vehicles is directly dependent on the quality and accuracy of the data they collect.

In this chapter, we will delve into the importance of data in autonomous vehicle development, discuss the various types of data collected by AVs, and explore the critical role of data preprocessing in training machine learning models. Finally, we will walk through a hands-on project that demonstrates how real-world data can be used to simulate driving conditions and help train self-driving systems.

1. The Importance of Data in AV Development

Data plays a crucial role in the development of self-driving cars, enabling them to perceive their environment, make decisions, and execute driving tasks. The more data an AV has, the better it can learn and improve its performance. This data not only includes raw sensor inputs but also annotations, labels, and contextual information that help AV systems understand the world.

1.1 The Role of Data in Perception

Perception is the ability of an AV to detect and understand objects in its environment. This is where the data collected from cameras, lidar, radar, and other sensors comes into play. These sensors capture data such as the distance to an object, its speed, and its type (pedestrian, vehicle, traffic sign, etc.). Perception algorithms use this raw data to create a "map" of the surrounding environment, which helps the car navigate and avoid obstacles.

- **Example:**
  The car's radar might detect an approaching vehicle at a certain distance, while cameras capture the vehicle's visual characteristics (make, model, color). The lidar system generates a 3D map of the surrounding area, including the road's geometry. All this data is combined to create a comprehensive understanding of the environment, which is then used to make real-time decisions.

1.2 The Role of Data in Decision-Making

Data also drives the decision-making process within AVs. After perceiving the environment, the vehicle's system must decide what to do next. Should it accelerate, brake, change lanes, or stop? The AV uses the data collected to make these decisions, often leveraging machine learning models trained on large datasets of driving experiences.

- **Example:**
  If a pedestrian is detected on the road, the AV must decide whether to stop, slow down, or continue driving. This decision is based on data such as the pedestrian's distance, movement speed, and intent (whether they are crossing the street or standing still).

1.3 The Role of Data in System Improvement

In addition to immediate decision-making, data is also used to improve the performance of self-driving systems over time. By collecting data from real-world driving experiences and using it to train machine learning models, AVs can continuously refine their ability to recognize objects, make decisions, and handle complex driving scenarios.

- **Example:**
  Data collected from real-world AV deployments, such as urban streets, highways, and rural roads, allows developers to identify common challenges (e.g., narrow roads, complex intersections) and train models to handle these scenarios more effectively.

2. Types of Data Collected by Autonomous Vehicles

Autonomous vehicles collect a wide variety of data from different sources, including sensors, cameras, GPS, and external environmental conditions. Each type of data serves a unique purpose in helping the AV understand its environment and navigate safely. Below are the primary types of data collected by self-driving cars:

2.1 Visual Data (Cameras)

Cameras provide high-resolution visual data that is used for object recognition, lane detection, traffic light recognition, and more. The visual data gathered by cameras is often in the form of RGB images or video streams, which are processed by computer vision algorithms to identify and track objects.

- **Example:**
  Cameras are used to detect pedestrians, vehicles, traffic signs, and other road markings. The visual data from cameras helps AVs make

decisions such as whether to yield, stop, or proceed through an intersection.

2.2 Sensor-Based Data (Radar, Lidar, Ultrasonic Sensors)

Autonomous vehicles also rely on radar, lidar, and ultrasonic sensors to collect data about the surrounding environment. These sensors help the vehicle perceive its surroundings in conditions where visual data might be insufficient, such as low light, fog, or rain.

1. **Radar:**
   Radar sensors emit radio waves to detect objects and measure their distance and speed. Radar is particularly useful for detecting large objects at long ranges, such as other vehicles.

2. **Lidar:**
   Lidar uses laser beams to measure distances and generate detailed, 3D maps of the environment. Lidar is particularly useful for creating precise spatial representations of the surroundings.

3. **Ultrasonic Sensors:**
   Ultrasonic sensors use sound waves to detect

nearby objects. They are commonly used for short-range tasks, such as parking assistance and low-speed maneuvering.

- **Example:**
  Radar might be used to detect an approaching vehicle at high speeds, while lidar can create a 3D map of the car's immediate environment, including pedestrians, road signs, and traffic lights.

2.3 Environmental Data (GPS, Weather, Road Conditions)

In addition to sensor data, AVs also rely on external environmental data to improve their performance. GPS provides the car with location data, while weather and road condition information can help the AV adjust its behavior to account for challenges like rain, snow, or icy roads.

1. **GPS:**
   GPS data helps AVs determine their location on a map and navigate to their destination. It is often used in conjunction with high-definition maps to enable precise localization.

2. **Weather Data:**
   Weather sensors provide information about environmental conditions, such as temperature, humidity, and visibility. This data helps AVs adjust their speed and driving behavior to account for changing weather conditions.

3. **Road Conditions:**
   Data about road conditions, such as potholes, construction zones, or icy patches, can be gathered through sensors or by receiving real-time updates from other vehicles or infrastructure.

- **Example:**
  If the weather data indicates that the road is icy, the vehicle may adjust its speed and following distance to maintain safety.

3. Data Preprocessing Techniques for Machine Learning

Once the data is collected by the vehicle's sensors, it must be processed before it can be used to train machine learning models. Data preprocessing is a critical step in ensuring that the data is clean, relevant, and formatted correctly for analysis.

3.1 Data Cleaning and Filtering

Raw data collected from sensors is often noisy or incomplete. Data cleaning involves removing irrelevant or erroneous data and filling in missing values. Filtering techniques can be applied to smooth out noise or reduce the impact of sensor errors.

- **Example:**
  If a radar sensor detects a false object due to interference, it must be filtered out before it can be used for decision-making. Similarly, data from cameras may need to be adjusted for lighting changes (e.g., shadows, glare) to ensure accurate object detection.

3.2 Data Normalization

Data normalization is the process of scaling the data to a standard range so that it can be effectively used by machine learning models. This is particularly important when dealing with sensor data, which can have different units and magnitudes.

- **Example:**
  In radar data, distances might be measured in meters, while camera data might be in pixel values. Normalizing the data ensures that the machine learning model treats all inputs equally and doesn't bias one sensor over another.

3.3 Feature Engineering

Feature engineering involves extracting relevant features from raw data to make it more suitable for machine learning algorithms. This might involve transforming the data into a form that the model can better understand, such as extracting edges from images or identifying key points in lidar data.

- **Example:**
  For object detection in images, feature engineering might involve detecting edges, corners, and textures, which help the model identify pedestrians or road signs more effectively.

3.4 Data Augmentation

Data augmentation is a technique used to artificially expand the dataset by generating modified versions of the original data. This can help improve the generalization ability of machine learning models by exposing them to a wider range of scenarios.

- **Example:**
  Data augmentation for image data might involve rotating, flipping, or cropping images to simulate different viewpoints, or adjusting brightness and contrast to account for different lighting conditions.

4. Hands-On: Using Real-World Data to Simulate Driving Conditions

To demonstrate how data is used in self-driving cars, let's walk through a simple project using real-world data to simulate driving conditions. This project will involve collecting data from a driving simulation environment, processing the data, and using it to train a machine learning model for object detection.

4.1 Setting Up the Simulation Environment

For this project, we will use a simulation platform like CARLA or LGSVL, which allows you to simulate real-world driving scenarios with virtual vehicles and environments. These platforms provide access to detailed sensor data, including camera images, lidar point clouds, and radar data.

1. **Install CARLA or LGSVL:**
   Set up the simulation environment on your computer by following the official installation instructions for CARLA or LGSVL.

2. **Collect Data:**
   Use the simulation environment to drive a virtual vehicle in different scenarios, such as city streets, highways, and intersections. Collect sensor data from the vehicle, including images, lidar scans, and radar readings.

4.2 Data Preprocessing for Machine Learning

Once the data is collected, preprocess it for machine learning. This might include cleaning the data, normalizing the features, and applying data augmentation techniques to generate more diverse training samples.

1. **Filter Noisy Data:**
   Remove any irrelevant data, such as outliers or sensor errors, and fill in missing values where necessary.

2. **Normalize the Data:**
   Scale the data from different sensors to a common range to ensure the machine learning model treats them equally.

3. **Augment the Data:**
   Apply transformations to simulate different driving conditions, such as varying lighting, weather, and object positions.

4.3 Training a Simple Object Detection Model

Next, use the preprocessed data to train a machine learning model for object detection. You can use a convolutional neural network (CNN) for this task, which is well-suited for image-based object recognition.

1. **Train the Model:**
   Using the augmented dataset, train a CNN to detect objects such as pedestrians, vehicles, and traffic signs. Use a tool like TensorFlow or PyTorch to build and train the model.

2. **Evaluate the Model:**

   Test the model on a separate validation dataset to evaluate its performance and adjust hyperparameters if necessary.

4.4 Testing the Model in a Simulation

Finally, test the trained model in the simulation environment to see how well it detects objects in real-time. Monitor the vehicle's behavior as it navigates through different scenarios and make any adjustments to the model as needed.

Conclusion

Data collection and processing are at the heart of autonomous vehicle development. The types of data collected—from visual and sensor-based data to environmental conditions—provide the foundation for enabling AVs to perceive their surroundings, make decisions, and navigate safely. Preprocessing this data effectively is essential for training machine learning models that allow AVs to improve over time. By working with real-world data in simulation environments, we can create more robust and intelligent self-driving systems that are ready for deployment in the real world.

Chapter 5: Perception Systems: How Autonomous Vehicles "See" the World

Introduction: Understanding Perception in Autonomous Vehicles

Perception is one of the fundamental capabilities that enable autonomous vehicles (AVs) to navigate and interact with their environment. Perception systems allow AVs to "see" the world in a way that mimics human sensory processing but with far more precision and adaptability. These systems use a combination of sensors, algorithms, and machine learning techniques to understand their surroundings and make decisions based on this understanding. Essentially, perception is how AVs transform raw sensory data into a representation of the world that allows them to perform tasks such as obstacle avoidance, object recognition, and path planning.

In the context of self-driving cars, perception involves the following key tasks:

- **Detection:** Identifying objects in the vehicle's environment (e.g., pedestrians, vehicles, traffic signs).

- **Classification:** Categorizing objects into different classes (e.g., car, bike, pedestrian).

- **Tracking:** Continuously monitoring the location and movement of objects.

- **Localization:** Determining the car's precise location in relation to its environment and mapping data.

In this chapter, we will explore the importance of perception in autonomous driving, the various sensors used to gather data for perception, and the techniques used for object detection and classification. Additionally, we will go through a practical tutorial on implementing basic object detection in Python.

1. Sensors and How They Contribute to Perception

Autonomous vehicles rely on a suite of sensors to gather data from their environment. Each sensor plays a unique role, and the data they generate is used to form a complete understanding of the world around the vehicle. Let's explore the different sensors typically used in AVs and how they contribute to the vehicle's perception system.

1.1 Cameras: Visual Perception

Cameras are one of the most important sensors in autonomous vehicles, providing visual data that enables the vehicle to "see" much like humans do. Cameras capture high-resolution images or video streams, which are processed by computer vision algorithms to recognize objects, detect road signs, and identify lane markings.

- **Applications in Perception:**
Cameras provide critical input for object detection, such as recognizing pedestrians, cyclists, other vehicles, and traffic signs. Additionally, they are used for lane detection and tracking other dynamic objects like cars in adjacent lanes. Cameras also play an essential role in identifying traffic signals, stop signs, and other road signs that influence the vehicle's decision-making.

- **Advantages of Cameras:**
Cameras provide rich visual data that can be interpreted to identify a wide range of objects. They are particularly effective in detecting features such as color, shape, and texture, which are important for identifying specific objects and road conditions.

- **Limitations:**
Cameras are highly dependent on environmental conditions such as lighting, weather, and visibility. In fog, rain, or at night, cameras may struggle to capture clear images, which is why they are usually paired with other sensors like radar or lidar for better robustness.

1.2 Lidar: Depth Perception

Lidar (Light Detection and Ranging) is a key sensor that uses laser light to create detailed, 3D maps of the environment. It measures the distance to objects by emitting laser pulses and recording the time it takes for the pulses to return. This allows lidar to capture the precise location of objects, making it an essential tool for depth perception.

- **Applications in Perception:**
  Lidar generates high-resolution, three-dimensional point clouds that provide accurate distance measurements of the surrounding environment. This allows AVs to detect obstacles, pedestrians, and vehicles with great precision, even in low visibility conditions. Lidar is particularly effective for detecting obstacles in the vehicle's path and for mapping the environment in 3D, which is crucial for navigation.

- **Advantages of Lidar:**
  Lidar provides precise distance measurements and is less affected by environmental lighting

conditions, making it a valuable sensor in challenging weather, such as fog or darkness.

- **Limitations:**
  Lidar is more expensive than cameras and radar, and its point clouds can sometimes be sparse, which can make it difficult to detect small or fast-moving objects. Additionally, lidar can have difficulty detecting certain materials, like glass or transparent objects.

1.3 Radar: Motion Detection and Object Tracking

Radar (Radio Detection and Ranging) is another important sensor used in AVs. It works by emitting radio waves that bounce off objects and return to the sensor. By measuring the time it takes for the waves to return, radar can determine the distance and speed of objects.

- **Applications in Perception:**
  Radar is primarily used for detecting large objects and tracking their motion, such as other vehicles. It is particularly effective in adverse weather conditions like rain, fog, or snow, where other sensors may struggle. Radar is also

used for adaptive cruise control, where the AV adjusts its speed to maintain a safe distance from the vehicle ahead.

- **Advantages of Radar:**
Radar is robust to environmental conditions like rain, snow, and fog, making it a valuable sensor for safe driving in poor visibility. It is also capable of detecting objects at longer ranges compared to cameras or lidar.

- **Limitations:**
Radar has relatively low resolution compared to lidar or cameras, so it may struggle to detect small objects or provide fine-grained details about the shape of obstacles.

1.4 Ultrasonic Sensors: Close-Range Detection

Ultrasonic sensors use high-frequency sound waves to detect objects at close range. These sensors are typically used for low-speed maneuvering, such as parking, and are effective for detecting objects in the immediate surroundings of the vehicle.

- **Applications in Perception:**
Ultrasonic sensors are used for parking assist

and object detection in tight spaces. They help the AV navigate in confined areas where other sensors might not be as effective, such as parking lots or when parallel parking.

- **Advantages of Ultrasonic Sensors:** They are inexpensive and simple to deploy, and they work well at close range (e.g., less than 5 meters).

- **Limitations:** Ultrasonic sensors have a limited range and can only detect objects in close proximity. They are also less effective at detecting objects that are moving at high speeds.

2. Object Detection and Classification Techniques

The data gathered from cameras, lidar, radar, and ultrasonic sensors must be processed to detect and classify objects in the vehicle's environment. Object detection and classification are crucial tasks in AV perception systems, as they allow the vehicle to identify objects (e.g., pedestrians, vehicles, traffic signs) and classify them into different categories.

2.1 Object Detection

Object detection is the process of identifying and locating objects within an image or point cloud. It is a critical step in enabling an AV to understand its environment and make decisions. In the case of cameras, object detection typically involves identifying the location of objects within an image, while lidar point clouds require detecting the position of objects in three-dimensional space.

- **Techniques for Object Detection:**

  - **Traditional Image Processing (Haar Cascades, HOG):**
    These are early techniques used for object detection based on feature extraction. Although less popular today, they laid the foundation for modern deep learning methods.

  - **Deep Learning (Convolutional Neural Networks - CNNs):**
    CNNs are the backbone of modern object detection techniques. They use layers of convolutional filters to automatically

learn features from the data, making them highly effective for detecting objects in images or video feeds. Popular frameworks for object detection using CNNs include Faster R-CNN, YOLO (You Only Look Once), and SSD (Single Shot MultiBox Detector).

2.2 Object Classification

Once objects have been detected, they need to be classified into different categories (e.g., car, pedestrian, cyclist). Classification involves assigning a label to each detected object based on its features.

- **Techniques for Object Classification:**

  - **CNNs for Classification:**
    After detection, CNNs are often used to classify objects based on their appearance. The network is trained on a labeled dataset that includes various object classes. The network learns to associate specific visual features with each class, allowing it to classify objects in real-time.

○ **Support Vector Machines (SVMs):**
SVMs are sometimes used as a classifier
after feature extraction, particularly in
older object detection systems.

---

3. Tutorial: Implementing Basic Object Detection in Python

Now that we have a foundational understanding of
object detection and classification, let's implement a
simple object detection system in Python using
OpenCV and a pre-trained deep learning model. In
this tutorial, we will use the YOLOv3 model for object
detection, which is a popular and efficient real-time
object detection system.

3.1 Setting Up the Environment

Before starting, make sure you have Python installed
on your system along with the following libraries:

- **OpenCV**: For image processing and handling
  video data.

- **NumPy**: For numerical operations.

- **TensorFlow/Keras** or **PyTorch**: For loading pre-trained models.

To install the necessary libraries, run:

bash

Copy

pip install opencv-python numpy tensorflow

3.2 Loading the YOLOv3 Model

For this tutorial, we will use a pre-trained YOLOv3 model. You can download the YOLOv3 weights and configuration file from the official YOLO website or GitHub repository. Once downloaded, use the following Python code to load the model.

python

Copy

```
import cv2

import numpy as np


# Load YOLO model

net = cv2.dnn.readNet("yolov3.weights", "yolov3.cfg")

layer_names = net.getLayerNames()
```

```python
output_layers = [layer_names[i-1] for i in
net.getUnconnectedOutLayers()]
```

3.3 Preprocessing the Input Image

To process an image for object detection, we need to convert the image into a format that the YOLO model can understand. This involves resizing the image, normalizing pixel values, and converting it into a blob.

python

Copy

```python
# Load the image
img = cv2.imread("input_image.jpg")
height, width, channels = img.shape


# Convert the image to a blob
blob = cv2.dnn.blobFromImage(img, 0.00392, (416, 416), (0, 0, 0), True, crop=False)

net.setInput(blob)
```

3.4 Running Object Detection

Once the image is prepared, we can run the YOLO model to detect objects. The model will output bounding boxes for each detected object along with its confidence score.

python

Copy

```python
# Get the model's output

outs = net.forward(output_layers)


# Loop through detections

for out in outs:

    for detection in out:

        scores = detection[5:]

        class_id = np.argmax(scores)

        confidence = scores[class_id]

        if confidence > 0.5:

            # Extract the bounding box

            center_x = int(detection[0] * width)

            center_y = int(detection[1] * height)

            w = int(detection[2] * width)
```

```python
h = int(detection[3] * height)


# Draw the bounding box

cv2.rectangle(img, (center_x - w // 2, center_y - h // 2), (center_x + w // 2, center_y + h // 2), (0, 255, 0), 2)
```

3.5 Displaying the Result

Finally, display the image with the detected objects.

python

Copy

```python
cv2.imshow("Object Detection", img)

cv2.waitKey(0)

cv2.destroyAllWindows()
```

Conclusion

Perception systems are at the heart of autonomous driving. They allow self-driving cars to "see" the world through a combination of sensors such as cameras, lidar, radar, and ultrasonic sensors. The data from these sensors is processed using object detection and classification techniques, enabling AVs to understand their surroundings and make real-time decisions. By using modern machine learning techniques such as deep learning and convolutional neural networks, AVs can achieve high levels of accuracy in identifying and classifying objects. In this chapter, we have also provided a practical tutorial on implementing basic object detection in Python, which serves as a foundation for more advanced autonomous vehicle applications.

Chapter 6: AI in Vehicle Control: How Cars Make Decisions

Introduction: The Role of AI in Making Decisions

Autonomous vehicles (AVs) have revolutionized the way we think about transportation. Unlike traditional vehicles that rely on human drivers to make split-second decisions, AVs must be able to make complex decisions in real-time, without human intervention. AI is at the heart of these decision-making systems, guiding AVs through dynamic environments while ensuring safety, efficiency, and adherence to traffic laws.

In this chapter, we will explore the critical role that AI plays in vehicle control, particularly in path planning, braking, and steering. We will discuss how reinforcement learning (RL) can be used to optimize decision-making processes, enabling AVs to adapt to changing road conditions, obstacles, and other dynamic elements in the environment. Finally, we will walk through a hands-on tutorial where we will build a simple path-planning algorithm to illustrate the decision-making process.

---

1. The Role of AI in Making Decisions

In autonomous vehicles, decision-making is a multifaceted process that involves multiple components working together to ensure smooth and safe operation. AI plays a critical role in all of these components, including path planning, braking, and steering. These decisions must be made in real-time, often in dynamic environments, where the vehicle must continuously adapt to new information from its sensors and the surrounding environment.

Let's break down the decision-making process into its key components:

1.1 Path Planning: Finding the Best Route

Path planning is one of the most fundamental aspects of an autonomous vehicle's decision-making process. It involves determining the most efficient and safe route for the vehicle to follow from its current position to the destination. This process can be divided into two parts:

1. **Global Path Planning:**
   This involves determining the overall route from the starting point to the destination, considering factors such as road types, speed limits, and turn instructions. It typically involves the use of high-definition maps, GPS, and traffic data.

2. **Local Path Planning:**
   Once the global path is determined, local path planning ensures that the vehicle can navigate through dynamic environments, such as intersections, construction zones, and crowded city streets. It involves real-time calculations to avoid obstacles, follow lane markings, and make decisions at intersections.

AI plays a key role in both global and local path planning by analyzing real-time data and optimizing the route based on the current conditions.

1.2 Braking: Stopping Safely

Braking is another crucial aspect of vehicle control that requires precise decision-making. In autonomous vehicles, braking decisions must be made based on several factors:

- **Obstacle Detection:** AI must determine when to apply the brakes to avoid collisions with pedestrians, vehicles, or other obstacles.

- **Distance and Speed:** The vehicle needs to analyze the distance to the vehicle in front and the relative speed to decide how much to decelerate or stop.

- **Traffic Signals:** AI also needs to decide when to stop for red lights or yield at intersections.

AI models are trained to take these factors into account, applying appropriate braking decisions in real-time.

1.3 Steering: Navigating the Road

Steering decisions in autonomous vehicles are equally important. AI systems must determine how to steer the vehicle in a way that ensures it stays within its lane, avoids obstacles, and follows the road's curvature. This includes:

- **Lane Keeping:** AI must detect lane markings and adjust the steering to keep the vehicle within its lane.

- **Turning:** When navigating corners, the vehicle must calculate the appropriate angle of steering based on the turn's radius and the vehicle's speed.

- **Merging:** AI must calculate the appropriate time and speed to merge into traffic lanes safely.

The vehicle's decision-making system uses real-time data from sensors like cameras and lidar to make precise steering adjustments.

2. Reinforcement Learning in Decision-Making Systems

Reinforcement learning (RL) is a branch of machine learning that is particularly useful in decision-making systems for autonomous vehicles. In RL, an agent (in this case, the autonomous vehicle) learns to make decisions by interacting with its environment and receiving feedback based on the actions it takes.

2.1 Understanding Reinforcement Learning

Reinforcement learning works by rewarding an agent for taking correct actions and penalizing it for taking wrong actions. Over time, the agent learns which actions lead to the highest cumulative rewards. In the context of autonomous vehicles, RL can help the vehicle learn optimal driving behaviors, such as when to brake, accelerate, or change lanes.

Key components of reinforcement learning in AVs include:

1. **Agent:** The AV itself, which takes actions and receives feedback.

2. **Environment:** The road network, obstacles, and other vehicles that the AV interacts with.

3. **Action:** The decisions made by the AV, such as accelerating, braking, or turning.

4. **Reward:** The feedback received after taking an action, which indicates whether the action was beneficial (positive reward) or harmful (negative reward).

5. **Policy:** The strategy the AV uses to determine the next action based on the current state.

2.2 Applications of Reinforcement Learning in Autonomous Vehicles

Reinforcement learning is particularly useful for optimizing complex driving tasks where explicit programming is not feasible. Below are some key applications of RL in autonomous vehicles:

- **Traffic Signal Prediction:** RL can help the AV predict traffic signal changes, allowing it to optimize stopping or starting decisions.

- **Merging and Lane Changing:** RL can be used to teach the vehicle when it is safe to change lanes or merge into traffic by learning from past experiences.

- **Adaptive Control Systems:** RL can improve braking and acceleration behavior, allowing the vehicle to adapt to different driving conditions, such as road surface quality or traffic congestion.

By using reinforcement learning, autonomous vehicles can learn from real-world experiences and improve their driving strategies over time, ultimately enhancing safety and efficiency.

---

3. Real-Time Decision-Making in Dynamic Environments

Autonomous vehicles must make decisions in real-time while navigating dynamic and often unpredictable environments. Unlike traditional vehicles that rely on human drivers to make split-second decisions, AVs must process vast amounts of sensory data and adjust their actions accordingly.

3.1 Dynamic Environments: Challenges and Considerations

The environment surrounding an autonomous vehicle is constantly changing. Some key factors that contribute to this dynamic nature include:

- **Traffic:** Other vehicles, pedestrians, cyclists, and road workers constantly move and change position, requiring constant adjustments from the AV.

- **Weather Conditions:** Rain, fog, and snow can obscure the vehicle's sensors and affect decision-making.

- **Unexpected Events:** Events like sudden road closures, accidents, or pedestrians crossing unexpectedly can require rapid decision-making.

- **Road Conditions:** Potholes, construction zones, and poor road markings can require the AV to adapt its path or speed.

To make real-time decisions, AVs rely on AI systems that process sensor data and make immediate decisions. These decisions must balance safety, efficiency, and compliance with traffic laws.

3.2 Decision-Making Frameworks in AVs

AVs rely on multiple layers of decision-making frameworks to handle different scenarios. These include:

- **Rule-Based Systems:** These systems follow pre-programmed rules, such as "stop at a red light" or "yield to pedestrians." While effective for basic decisions, they lack flexibility in more complex scenarios.

- **Model Predictive Control (MPC):** MPC is a control strategy that involves predicting future states of the vehicle based on its current trajectory. It is used for optimizing path planning and making decisions based on future predictions, such as avoiding collisions.

- **Deep Reinforcement Learning (DRL):** DRL combines the strengths of deep learning and reinforcement learning to enable the vehicle to learn from experience and make decisions based on long-term rewards.

The integration of these frameworks allows AVs to make decisions in dynamic environments while continuously learning and improving.

4. Hands-On: Building a Simple Path-Planning Algorithm

To help solidify the concepts covered, let's build a simple path-planning algorithm for a simulated autonomous vehicle. We'll use basic AI techniques to create an algorithm that can navigate a predefined map and avoid obstacles.

4.1 Setting Up the Environment

To get started, we need to set up a Python environment with the necessary libraries:

- **Numpy** for numerical operations.

- **Matplotlib** for visualization.

- **SciPy** for path optimization.

You can install the required libraries using pip:

bash

Copy

pip install numpy matplotlib scipy

4.2 Defining the Grid Map

In this example, we'll create a simple grid map to simulate the environment. The map will consist of a grid where each cell represents a position the vehicle can occupy. The vehicle must navigate from a starting point to a goal, avoiding obstacles.

python

Copy

```python
import numpy as np

import matplotlib.pyplot as plt


# Create a 10x10 grid map

grid_size = 10

grid = np.zeros((grid_size, grid_size))


# Define obstacles
```

```
grid[3:6, 3:6] = 1  # Obstacles in the center


# Define start and goal positions

start = (0, 0)

goal = (9, 9)


# Plot the grid

plt.imshow(grid, cmap='gray')

plt.scatter(start[1], start[0], color='green',
label='Start')

plt.scatter(goal[1], goal[0], color='red', label='Goal')

plt.legend()

plt.show()
```

4.3 Path Planning Algorithm

We'll use the A* (A-star) algorithm, a popular path-planning algorithm for finding the shortest path in a grid. The A* algorithm works by evaluating each possible path and selecting the one with the lowest cost, considering both distance and obstacles.

python

Copy

```python
import heapq


# Define the A* algorithm
def astar(grid, start, goal):
    open_list = []
    closed_list = set()
    heapq.heappush(open_list, (0, start))


    # Dictionary to store the path
    came_from = {}


    # Cost from start to current node
    g_cost = {start: 0}


    # Estimated cost from current node to goal
    f_cost = {start: heuristic(start, goal)}
```

```
while open_list:

    _, current = heapq.heappop(open_list)


    if current == goal:

        return reconstruct_path(came_from, current)


    closed_list.add(current)


    for neighbor in get_neighbors(current, grid):

        if neighbor in closed_list:

            continue


        tentative_g_cost = g_cost[current] + 1


        if neighbor not in g_cost or tentative_g_cost < g_cost[neighbor]:

            came_from[neighbor] = current
```

```
            g_cost[neighbor] = tentative_g_cost

            f_cost[neighbor] = g_cost[neighbor] +
heuristic(neighbor, goal)

            heapq.heappush(open_list, (f_cost[neighbor],
neighbor))


    return []


# Define heuristic function (Manhattan distance)
def heuristic(a, b):
    return abs(a[0] - b[0]) + abs(a[1] - b[1])


# Get neighbors of the current node
def get_neighbors(node, grid):
    neighbors = []
    x, y = node
    for dx, dy in [(-1, 0), (1, 0), (0, -1), (0, 1)]:
        nx, ny = x + dx, y + dy
```

```python
        if 0 <= nx < grid.shape[0] and 0 <= ny <
grid.shape[1] and grid[nx, ny] == 0:

            neighbors.append((nx, ny))

    return neighbors


# Reconstruct the path from the goal to the start

def reconstruct_path(came_from, current):

    path = [current]

    while current in came_from:

        current = came_from[current]

        path.append(current)

    path.reverse()

    return path


# Run the A* algorithm to find the path

path = astar(grid, start, goal)


# Plot the path
```

```
for (x, y) in path:

    plt.scatter(y, x, color='blue', s=10)

plt.imshow(grid, cmap='gray')

plt.scatter(start[1], start[0], color='green',
label='Start')

plt.scatter(goal[1], goal[0], color='red', label='Goal')

plt.legend()

plt.show()
```

4.4 Explanation of the Algorithm

In this hands-on section, we implemented a simple A*
algorithm for path planning. Here's a breakdown of
the process:

- **Grid Representation:**
  The environment is represented as a 10x10 grid,
  where 0 indicates an empty cell and 1 indicates
  an obstacle.

- *A Algorithm:**
  The algorithm starts at the initial position and
  explores neighboring cells, calculating the cost
  to reach each cell. It uses a heuristic

(Manhattan distance) to estimate the cost to the goal. The algorithm continues until it reaches the goal or finds the optimal path.

Conclusion

AI in vehicle control is a critical aspect of autonomous driving. From path planning to braking and steering, AI systems enable vehicles to make real-time decisions that ensure safety and efficiency. Reinforcement learning plays a crucial role in optimizing decision-making systems, allowing vehicles to learn from experience and improve over time. By simulating dynamic environments and employing decision-making frameworks like A*, autonomous vehicles can navigate complex roadways safely and effectively.

This chapter has covered key concepts of vehicle control in AVs, including the role of AI, reinforcement learning, and real-time decision-making. The hands-on tutorial on path planning demonstrated the application of AI in making decisions, providing a foundation for more advanced autonomous driving techniques.

Chapter 7: Simulations and Testing: The Virtual Road to Real-World Deployment

Introduction: The Importance of Testing AVs in Virtual Environments

Testing autonomous vehicles (AVs) in virtual environments has become a crucial step in ensuring their safety, reliability, and performance before real-world deployment. The complexity of driving in real-world conditions—where vehicles must deal with pedestrians, unexpected obstacles, variable weather conditions, and other dynamic factors—makes it nearly impossible to test AVs in a purely physical environment. Furthermore, the cost of testing physical prototypes and the potential risks to public safety make it necessary to first simulate various driving scenarios in controlled, virtual settings.

Simulations offer a safe, cost-effective way to test and refine AV systems, particularly when it comes to perception, decision-making, and control algorithms. These environments allow developers to simulate a wide variety of conditions, from urban streets to rural highways, to complex traffic situations. Virtual testing environments also enable the rapid iteration of AV software, making it possible to perform thousands of tests in a matter of hours—something that would take months or even years in the real world.

In this chapter, we will explore the key reasons why virtual testing is critical for AV development, the tools and platforms available for simulating AV scenarios, the step-by-step process of testing AV software in simulations, and a hands-on project demonstrating how to run a simple AV simulation using the CARLA platform.

1. The Role of Virtual Testing in AV Development

Virtual testing plays a critical role in the development cycle of autonomous vehicles by offering several key benefits:

1.1 Safety and Risk Reduction

Simulations allow developers to test AVs in a risk-free environment. Testing in real-world conditions often involves high risks, especially in early stages of development when the vehicle's systems may not yet be fully refined. By using virtual environments, AV developers can run scenarios that might be too dangerous or impractical to test in the physical world, such as extreme weather conditions, accidents, or unpredictable pedestrian behavior. These tests help identify potential hazards and improve the system's ability to respond to them before deploying the vehicle in public spaces.

1.2 Scalability and Efficiency

In real-world testing, it is difficult to account for every possible scenario, and testing is time-consuming. With simulations, thousands of different driving scenarios can be generated and tested within a short amount of time. This scalability ensures that AV systems are exposed to a broader range of conditions than they would ever encounter on the road. Furthermore, since simulations allow for rapid testing and iteration, developers can identify bugs or flaws in the software quickly and refine their systems accordingly.

1.3 Cost-Effectiveness

The cost of building and maintaining physical testing environments, such as closed tracks or controlled cities, can be prohibitively expensive. Virtual environments eliminate the need for expensive infrastructure, allowing developers to test their systems without incurring significant costs. Moreover, simulations reduce the wear and tear on physical vehicles, which can be costly to maintain over time.

1.4 Reproducibility and Data Collection

One of the most powerful advantages of virtual testing is the ability to reproduce scenarios exactly, which is crucial for debugging and improving AV systems. Virtual simulations allow developers to replay specific situations and analyze the vehicle's response in detail. This level of reproducibility and data collection is invaluable for fine-tuning algorithms, optimizing performance, and ensuring that AVs respond consistently in real-world situations.

---

2. Tools and Platforms for Simulating AV Scenarios

Several tools and platforms have been developed specifically to simulate autonomous vehicle scenarios. These platforms provide realistic environments and scenarios to test AV systems in a controlled, virtual space. Below are some of the most widely used simulation platforms:

2.1 CARLA (Car Learning to Act)

CARLA is an open-source simulator specifically designed for the development, training, and validation of autonomous driving systems. It is widely regarded as one of the most realistic and flexible simulation platforms for AV development. CARLA provides a range of features that make it an ideal tool for testing AV algorithms:

- **Realistic Environment:** CARLA allows for highly detailed urban and rural environments, including various types of weather, day/night cycles, and road conditions.

- **Customizable Scenarios:** Developers can design custom scenarios, such as traffic patterns, roadworks, or pedestrian behaviors, to evaluate how AVs respond in specific situations.

- **Sensor Integration:** CARLA supports integration with a variety of sensors commonly used in autonomous vehicles, such as cameras, lidar, radar, and GPS.

- **Open-Source:** CARLA's open-source nature allows developers to modify the platform to suit their needs, contributing to its popularity among research institutions and developers.

2.2 LGSVL Simulator

The LGSVL Simulator is another widely used simulation platform that offers realistic testing environments for autonomous vehicles. LGSVL supports integration with popular autonomous driving stacks, such as Apollo and Autoware, and provides a range of tools for testing AV systems:

- **High-Fidelity Environments:** LGSVL offers detailed simulations with real-time traffic and pedestrian movement, as well as customizable weather conditions.

- **Integration with ROS (Robot Operating System):** LGSVL integrates seamlessly with ROS, allowing developers to run simulations using real-world robot software and algorithms.

- **Autonomous Driving Stack Support:** It is designed to work with various AV stacks, making it ideal for testing complex decision-making algorithms.

2.3 SUMO (Simulation of Urban Mobility)

SUMO is an open-source traffic simulation tool designed for modeling large-scale road networks. While it is not as focused on AV-specific testing as CARLA or LGSVL, it can still be used in conjunction with other platforms to simulate traffic flow and vehicle interactions. SUMO is widely used in academic research and transportation studies to simulate traffic patterns and evaluate transportation policies.

2.4 VISSIM

VISSIM is a commercial traffic simulation tool used for modeling and analyzing traffic flow in urban environments. It is particularly useful for simulating large-scale traffic networks, including vehicles, pedestrians, and public transport. VISSIM is often used for traffic planning and optimization, but it can also be adapted for AV testing by integrating it with other AV development platforms.

2.5 Other Tools: ROS/Gazebo

ROS (Robot Operating System) is a popular framework for building and testing robotic systems, and Gazebo is a simulation platform often used in conjunction with ROS for simulating environments and robotic movements. While not designed specifically for AVs, the combination of ROS and Gazebo can be used for autonomous vehicle testing by simulating realistic environments and integrating AV control algorithms.

3. The Process of Testing AV Software in Simulation

Testing autonomous vehicle software in simulations involves several stages, from scenario creation to evaluation of system performance. The following outlines the typical process of testing AV software in simulation:

3.1 Scenario Creation and Customization

The first step in simulation testing is creating and customizing scenarios that mimic real-world driving conditions. Developers can define the environment, traffic flow, road conditions, and other dynamic factors to simulate a variety of situations. Common scenarios include:

- **Urban Driving:** Simulating a vehicle navigating through busy city streets, dealing with pedestrians, cyclists, and other vehicles.

- **Highway Driving:** Testing AV performance on highways, focusing on lane changes, speed regulation, and adaptive cruise control.

- **Extreme Weather Conditions:** Simulating rainy, snowy, or foggy weather to test how the AV's perception and decision-making algorithms handle low-visibility conditions.

- **Emergency Situations:** Simulating situations such as sudden pedestrian crossings, road closures, or unexpected obstacles in the vehicle's path.

3.2 Sensor Data Integration

Once the scenarios are created, the next step is to integrate sensor data into the simulation. Sensors such as cameras, lidar, radar, and GPS are used to collect environmental data, which is then fed into the AV software. This data helps the vehicle perceive its surroundings, make decisions, and control its movements.

- **Perception System Testing:** Simulating different sensor inputs allows developers to test the perception system's ability to detect and classify objects in various conditions. For example, testing the AV's ability to detect a pedestrian in the middle of the street under low-light conditions.

- **Sensor Fusion:** Testing how data from different sensors, such as lidar and radar, is fused to create a coherent understanding of the environment.

3.3 Algorithm and Software Integration

Once the sensors are set up, the next step is integrating the AV's decision-making algorithms, such as path planning, control, and decision-making. This is where the AV software interacts with the simulated environment, and the vehicle must make real-time decisions based on the sensory data it receives.

- **Path Planning:** Testing the vehicle's ability to plan its route through various scenarios, such as choosing the optimal lane on a highway or navigating a complex intersection.

- **Control Systems:** Testing the vehicle's ability to steer, brake, and accelerate based on its path and the surrounding environment.

3.4 Simulation Execution and Data Collection

With the simulation environment fully set up, the AV software is executed within the simulation platform. During execution, the simulation collects data on various performance metrics, such as:

- **Safety Metrics:** How well the vehicle avoids collisions and maintains safe distances from other vehicles.

- **Efficiency Metrics:** How efficiently the vehicle navigates its path and adheres to traffic rules, such as speed limits and traffic signal adherence.

- **Sensor Accuracy:** The accuracy of the perception system in detecting and classifying objects.

3.5 Evaluation and Debugging

After the simulation runs, developers evaluate the performance of the AV software based on the data collected. Any issues or unexpected behaviors are identified, and adjustments are made to the system. This process is repeated iteratively to improve the software's performance and ensure it meets safety and efficiency standards.

- **Identifying Edge Cases:** Simulations can be used to identify edge cases—rare or unusual situations that the AV might encounter on the road. These can include interactions with pedestrians, cyclists, or erratic drivers.

---

4. Project: Running a Simple AV Simulation Using CARLA

Let's now walk through a simple project where we run an autonomous vehicle simulation using the CARLA simulator. This project will guide you through setting up the CARLA environment, running a basic simulation, and testing an AV's decision-making capabilities.

4.1 Setting Up CARLA

To begin, download and install CARLA from the official repository (https://github.com/carla-simulator/carla). CARLA is available for Windows and Linux, and detailed installation instructions are provided on the CARLA website.

Once installed, you can launch the CARLA simulator and access its environment via Python API or directly through the graphical interface.

4.2 Running the Simulation

After setting up CARLA, let's run a simple simulation where an AV navigates through an urban environment, avoiding obstacles and obeying traffic signals. Here is a basic Python script to control the AV using CARLA's API:

python

Copy

```
import carla
```

```python
# Connect to the CARLA server

client = carla.Client('localhost', 2000)

world = client.get_world()


# Set up the vehicle and sensors

blueprint =
world.get_blueprint_library().filter('model3')[0]

spawn_point = carla.Transform(carla.Location(x=0,
y=0, z=0))

vehicle = world.spawn_actor(blueprint, spawn_point)


# Set up the camera for visualization

camera_bp =
world.get_blueprint_library().find('sensor.camera.rgb')

camera_transform =
carla.Transform(carla.Location(x=2, y=0, z=1))

camera = world.spawn_actor(camera_bp,
camera_transform, attach_to=vehicle)
```

Start the simulation

```
vehicle.apply_control(carla.VehicleControl(throttle=1.
0, steer=0.0))
```

4.3 Testing the AV's Decision-Making

In the simulation, the AV will begin driving and make basic decisions like accelerating and steering. The next step is to integrate sensors such as cameras and lidar for perception, allowing the vehicle to detect obstacles and adjust its trajectory in real-time.

You can create more complex decision-making systems by integrating path-planning algorithms or reinforcement learning models into the simulation.

4.4 Evaluating the Performance

After running the simulation, analyze how well the AV performed in navigating the environment. You can visualize the sensor data and evaluate the vehicle's ability to avoid obstacles, obey traffic signals, and stay within its lane.

Conclusion

Simulations and testing are indispensable for developing autonomous vehicles, offering a safe, scalable, and cost-effective way to refine AV systems before deployment in the real world. By using platforms like CARLA and LGSVL, developers can test a wide range of driving scenarios and improve the safety, efficiency, and reliability of their AVs. The hands-on project demonstrated how CARLA can be used to simulate driving environments, making it easier for developers to test and evaluate AV decision-making algorithms.

As AV technologies continue to evolve, simulations will play an even larger role in advancing these systems, ultimately paving the way for the widespread deployment of autonomous vehicles. Through extensive virtual testing, we can ensure that AVs are ready for the complex and dynamic challenges they will face on the road.

Chapter 8: Challenges in Autonomous Vehicle Development

Introduction

The development of autonomous vehicles (AVs) is one of the most transformative technological advancements of the 21st century. AVs promise to revolutionize transportation by making it safer, more efficient, and accessible. However, their development is fraught with challenges—technical, ethical, legal, and societal. These challenges must be addressed before AVs can be fully integrated into society and achieve their potential.

In this chapter, we will explore the major challenges developers face when creating autonomous vehicles, ranging from the complexities of sensor fusion and real-time processing to ethical concerns surrounding liability and public trust. We will also examine how developers are working to overcome these challenges and make self-driving technology a reality.

1. Technical Challenges

The technical challenges involved in the development of autonomous vehicles are vast and complex. These challenges must be overcome for AVs to safely and effectively navigate the world.

1.1 Sensor Fusion: Integrating Data from Multiple Sources

One of the most significant technical challenges in AV development is sensor fusion—the process of combining data from multiple sensors, such as cameras, lidar, radar, and ultrasonic sensors, to create a cohesive understanding of the environment. Each sensor has its strengths and weaknesses, and no single sensor can provide the comprehensive view of the surroundings that an AV needs to make informed decisions.

- **Cameras** provide high-resolution visual data, ideal for object recognition and understanding of the road environment, but they struggle in poor lighting or adverse weather conditions.

- **Lidar** offers precise 3D spatial data, which helps in accurately mapping the environment and detecting objects, but its range is typically limited compared to radar.

- **Radar** excels in detecting objects in low-visibility conditions, such as fog, rain, or snow, but it provides lower-resolution data compared to lidar and cameras.

- **Ultrasonic sensors** are useful for short-range detection, such as in parking or maneuvering, but their limited range makes them unsuitable for detecting objects at a distance.

The challenge is not just in collecting data from these various sensors but in integrating this data effectively. Sensor fusion algorithms must combine the data from all these sensors in real-time, creating an accurate and cohesive model of the vehicle's environment. This integration must also be highly reliable, as any failure to detect and accurately interpret the surrounding world could lead to catastrophic consequences.

- **Solution Approach:**
  Developers are using advanced machine learning models, particularly deep learning techniques, to improve sensor fusion. By training models on large datasets from various sensors, they can learn how to handle conflicting or incomplete data and make decisions based on the most reliable sensor inputs. New approaches, like multi-modal fusion, are being explored, where data from sensors are combined at different stages to ensure the most accurate output.

1.2 Real-Time Processing: Making Decisions in Milliseconds

Autonomous vehicles must make decisions in real-time, often in dynamic environments where conditions can change in fractions of a second. Whether it's detecting an obstacle, calculating the best route, or adjusting speed to maintain safety, these decisions need to be made with minimal latency. The AV's computer system must process and analyze vast amounts of sensor data instantly to make informed decisions.

- **Challenges:**
  Real-time processing in AVs is computationally intensive. Each sensor, such as cameras, lidar, and radar, generates massive amounts of data, which must be processed in real-time to make decisions. If the system experiences any delays, the vehicle may fail to react in time, leading to potential accidents. The vehicle must also make decisions that balance speed, safety, and comfort, all while adhering to traffic laws.

- **Solution Approach:**
  Developers are investing in high-performance computing hardware and software to enable real-time processing. Edge computing is also becoming a key solution, where computing tasks are offloaded to devices closer to the sensors (i.e., onboard the vehicle), reducing latency and enabling faster decision-making. AI models are also being optimized for real-time inference, allowing the AV to process and act on sensor data in milliseconds.

1.3 Edge Computing: Processing Data Locally for Faster Decision-Making

Edge computing refers to processing data closer to where it is generated—on the vehicle itself—rather than sending the data to remote servers for analysis. This is critical in autonomous vehicles, where low-latency, real-time decisions are essential for safe operation.

- **Challenges:**
  Autonomous vehicles generate vast amounts of data from sensors and cameras, and sending all of this data to a central server for processing would introduce significant delays. Additionally, a robust internet connection may not always be available, particularly in remote areas or during high-traffic events. For AVs to make decisions without relying on cloud-based systems, they need powerful edge computing systems onboard.

- **Solution Approach:**
  Companies are developing powerful onboard computing systems, often based on custom hardware (e.g., NVIDIA DRIVE, Intel Mobileye),

which can process vast amounts of data in real time. These systems use specialized AI chips to accelerate machine learning algorithms, enabling real-time decision-making without relying on external servers.

---

2. Ethical and Legal Challenges

While the technical challenges of AV development are substantial, there are also significant ethical and legal issues that must be addressed. These challenges focus on the responsibility, accountability, and legal implications of AV decisions.

2.1 Liability: Who is Responsible for an Accident Involving an AV?

One of the most pressing legal questions in autonomous vehicle development is liability—who is responsible if an AV is involved in an accident? In traditional vehicles, the human driver is responsible for making decisions and controlling the vehicle. However, in an autonomous vehicle, the vehicle's AI system makes these decisions. This raises questions about who should be held accountable in the event of a crash: the manufacturer, the software developer, or the vehicle owner?

- **Challenges:**
  Determining liability in the case of accidents involving autonomous vehicles is complicated. Traditional traffic laws and insurance models were designed with human drivers in mind and may not apply directly to AVs. Furthermore, AVs rely on machine learning and AI systems that are constantly evolving. This creates challenges in ensuring that the vehicle's AI can be held accountable for its decisions.

- **Solution Approach:**
  Developers and regulators are working together to establish clear frameworks for liability. This may involve revising existing traffic laws, creating new insurance models for AVs, and implementing tracking systems to monitor how AVs make decisions during driving. Many legal experts suggest that liability should be shared among the vehicle manufacturer, the software developer, and the owner, depending on the circumstances of the accident.

2.2 Safety: Ensuring the Reliability and Safety of AV Systems

Safety is the primary concern in the development of autonomous vehicles. AVs must meet rigorous safety standards to ensure they can operate in diverse environments without causing harm to passengers, pedestrians, or other road users.

- **Challenges:**
  Developing autonomous vehicle systems that are safe enough to operate in complex, unpredictable real-world environments is an enormous challenge. AVs must be able to handle emergency situations, navigate through traffic, and respond to unexpected road conditions, all while adhering to traffic laws. Even a minor flaw in the AV's system could result in an accident.

- **Solution Approach:**
  Developers use a combination of rigorous simulation testing, real-world testing, and safety protocols to ensure the safety of AVs. Many manufacturers follow safety standards set by organizations such as the Society of Automotive Engineers (SAE) and National

Highway Traffic Safety Administration (NHTSA). Additionally, ongoing updates and testing of AV systems are necessary to address safety concerns continually.

2.3 Regulatory Compliance: Navigating the Legal Landscape for AVs

As autonomous vehicles become more advanced, regulatory bodies around the world are working to develop appropriate frameworks to govern their use. These regulations need to address a wide range of concerns, including safety, insurance, traffic laws, and data privacy.

- **Challenges:**
  The regulatory environment for autonomous vehicles is still evolving. Different countries and regions have different rules and standards, and some may be more supportive of AV development than others. AV developers must navigate this complex landscape, ensuring that their vehicles meet local and international standards. Furthermore, AV systems must comply with data privacy laws, as they collect

vast amounts of data about their surroundings and passengers.

- **Solution Approach:**
  Developers are working closely with regulatory agencies to ensure that AVs meet safety standards and adhere to local laws. Many AV manufacturers have established collaborations with governments to shape future regulations. Additionally, AVs are being designed with built-in compliance features, such as data encryption, to protect user privacy.

3. Social Challenges

The introduction of autonomous vehicles into society raises several social challenges, particularly related to public trust, job displacement, and the potential societal impacts of AVs.

3.1 Public Trust: Overcoming Skepticism and Concerns

One of the most significant social challenges for AVs is gaining public trust. Many people are skeptical about the safety and reliability of autonomous vehicles, particularly when it comes to trusting AI systems to make critical decisions in real-time.

- **Challenges:**
  Public concern about the safety and reliability of AVs is fueled by accidents involving self-driving vehicles, as well as general apprehension about the ability of machines to make life-or-death decisions. Despite the potential benefits of AVs, such as reducing traffic accidents and increasing mobility, many people remain wary of putting their lives in the hands of an AI system.

- **Solution Approach:**
  Developers and manufacturers are working to build trust by focusing on safety, transparency, and education. By conducting rigorous testing, releasing detailed safety reports, and showing the real-world benefits of AVs (such as reduced accidents and improved traffic flow), manufacturers aim to convince the public that AVs are safe and reliable. Additionally, improving the technology and ensuring that AV systems are robust and fault-tolerant will help alleviate public concerns.

3.2 Job Displacement: The Impact on Employment

The widespread adoption of autonomous vehicles is likely to lead to significant changes in the job market. Many industries, such as transportation, logistics, and delivery services, rely heavily on human drivers. As AVs become more common, millions of jobs in these sectors could be displaced.

- **Challenges:**
  The potential for job displacement is a major concern, as many workers may find themselves without employment opportunities.
  Additionally, the transition to an AV-dominated workforce may create new social and economic disparities. The rise of autonomous vehicles may exacerbate income inequality if workers displaced by automation do not have the necessary skills to transition into new roles.

- **Solution Approach:**
  Developers, governments, and educational institutions must work together to create programs that can help workers transition into new roles. Reskilling programs, career transitions, and job creation in the tech sector

could help mitigate the impact of job loss. Additionally, AV developers are exploring ways to collaborate with industries to create new job opportunities related to AV maintenance, software development, and fleet management.

4. Case Study: How Developers are Overcoming These Challenges

To illustrate how developers are addressing the challenges faced in AV development, let's look at the efforts of one of the leading companies in the field: Waymo.

Waymo, the self-driving car division of Alphabet (Google's parent company), has been at the forefront of AV development. It has made significant strides in overcoming the technical challenges of sensor fusion and real-time decision-making by developing a robust software stack capable of processing data from multiple sensors and making complex decisions in real-time. Through extensive testing, both in simulations and on public roads, Waymo has demonstrated the potential of AV technology to operate safely in diverse environments.

On the regulatory side, Waymo has worked closely with government agencies and regulators to ensure compliance with safety standards and to help shape the future of autonomous vehicle laws. In terms of public trust, Waymo has prioritized transparency by publishing safety reports and participating in public demonstrations to show that their vehicles are capable of operating safely and efficiently.

In addressing the social challenges of job displacement, Waymo has partnered with organizations to support workers who may be affected by automation. It has also emphasized the creation of new jobs in areas like AV maintenance, software engineering, and vehicle fleet management.

Conclusion

The road to widespread deployment of autonomous vehicles is fraught with challenges—technical, ethical, legal, and social. These challenges must be addressed before AVs can be safely and efficiently integrated into society. However, through ongoing research, testing, and collaboration between developers, regulators, and society at large, significant progress is being made. By overcoming these hurdles, we can look forward to a future where autonomous vehicles contribute to a safer, more efficient, and sustainable transportation system.

This chapter has explored the multifaceted challenges involved in AV development and highlighted how developers and stakeholders are actively working to overcome them. By addressing these challenges head-on, autonomous vehicles have the potential to transform our transportation systems, improving mobility and safety for all.

Chapter 9: AI and Robotics in Vehicle Manufacturing

Introduction: The Role of AI and Robotics in Revolutionizing Vehicle Manufacturing

The automotive industry has been at the forefront of manufacturing innovation for decades. The integration of artificial intelligence (AI) and robotics in vehicle manufacturing has accelerated this transformation, enabling unprecedented levels of precision, efficiency, and customization. AI and robotics have not only optimized traditional manufacturing processes but also unlocked entirely new capabilities that are reshaping the future of automotive production.

This chapter explores the impact of AI and robotics on vehicle manufacturing, focusing on automation in assembly lines, the rise of collaborative robots (cobots), and the practical applications of robotics in manufacturing. Additionally, we will provide a hands-on project that demonstrates the basics of programming a robot arm for assembly tasks, giving readers practical knowledge on how robotics are programmed to perform real-world manufacturing functions.

1. The Impact of AI and Robotics on Vehicle Manufacturing

The automotive industry has long relied on automation to streamline production processes. However, with the advancement of AI and robotics, manufacturers are now able to take automation to the next level. These technologies are improving nearly every aspect of vehicle manufacturing, from the assembly line to quality control, logistics, and even customer customization.

1.1 Precision and Efficiency in Manufacturing

AI and robotics have significantly enhanced the precision and efficiency of vehicle manufacturing. Robots are capable of performing repetitive tasks with consistent accuracy, reducing the likelihood of human error. This is particularly important in automotive production, where even small errors can result in significant issues in the final product.

- **Example:** In welding, robots can weld car parts with much higher precision and speed than human workers, ensuring stronger, more durable joints in vehicle frames. AI-powered vision systems also allow robots to adjust their movements in real-time to accommodate variations in parts, ensuring that even complex geometries are manufactured correctly.

1.2 Speed and Scalability in Production

The ability to produce vehicles faster and at a larger scale is one of the key benefits of AI and robotics in manufacturing. Automated systems can work around the clock without the need for breaks or rest, allowing manufacturers to meet high demand without sacrificing quality.

- **Example:** Autonomous robots are used in car body assembly lines, where they perform tasks such as lifting heavy parts, aligning components, and fastening bolts. These robots can work faster than human workers, speeding up the production process without compromising safety or quality.

1.3 Customization and Flexibility

As demand for customized vehicles continues to grow, AI and robotics are helping manufacturers meet these needs by enabling more flexible production lines. AI algorithms can analyze customer preferences and help design vehicles that meet specific requirements, while robots can be reprogrammed to handle a variety of tasks on the same production line.

- **Example:** Robots in automotive assembly lines can switch between different models or configurations of vehicles without the need for extensive retooling. This flexibility is particularly important in meeting the growing demand for personalized vehicles, such as custom interiors or special features.

2. Automation in Assembly Lines: Benefits and Challenges

The automation of assembly lines has been a key factor in increasing the efficiency and productivity of vehicle manufacturing. However, while the benefits of automation are clear, there are also challenges associated with implementing these systems.

2.1 Benefits of Automation in Assembly Lines

The shift toward automation in vehicle manufacturing has led to several benefits, including increased production speed, improved quality, and enhanced worker safety. Some of the key benefits are:

- **Increased Production Speed:** Robots can work faster than human workers, allowing for a significant increase in production rates. For instance, a robotic arm can perform a task such as assembling an engine part or installing a windshield in a fraction of the time it would take a human to do the same task.

- **Improved Quality Control:** Automated systems are programmed to perform tasks with high precision, reducing the likelihood of defects.

This improves the overall quality of the vehicle and reduces the risk of costly recalls or repairs.

- **Enhanced Safety:** Robots are used in high-risk environments, such as welding, painting, and heavy lifting. By automating these tasks, manufacturers can reduce the risk of workplace injuries and provide a safer environment for human workers.

2.2 Challenges in Automation

While the benefits of automation are substantial, implementing robotic systems in assembly lines also presents certain challenges:

- **Initial Investment Costs:** Setting up automated systems in manufacturing plants requires significant upfront investment in robotics, AI software, and infrastructure. This can be a barrier for smaller manufacturers or those with limited resources.

- **Integration with Legacy Systems:** Many automotive manufacturers rely on legacy systems that were not designed for automation. Integrating new robotic systems with these older systems can be complex and time-consuming.

- **Workforce Transition:** As robots take over more tasks, there is a potential for job displacement. Manufacturers must invest in retraining programs to help workers transition to new roles that require different skills, such as programming and maintaining robotic systems.

3. Collaborative Robots (Cobots) in Manufacturing

Collaborative robots, or cobots, are designed to work alongside human workers in a shared workspace. Unlike traditional industrial robots, which are often isolated from humans for safety reasons, cobots are built with safety features that allow them to operate alongside human workers without the need for physical barriers.

3.1 The Role of Cobots in Automotive Manufacturing

Cobots are increasingly being used in automotive manufacturing to assist workers in tasks that require dexterity, flexibility, and human judgment. These robots are typically used for tasks that are physically demanding or repetitive, allowing human workers to focus on higher-level tasks.

- **Example:** In a vehicle assembly line, a cobot might assist a worker in lifting and positioning heavy parts, such as a car door or engine block. The cobot can hold the part in place while the worker fastens bolts, improving both speed and safety.

3.2 Advantages of Cobots

The integration of cobots into manufacturing lines offers several advantages:

- **Increased Productivity:** Cobots can work in tandem with human workers, increasing the speed and efficiency of the production process without sacrificing safety or quality.

- **Improved Ergonomics:** Cobots can take on repetitive or physically demanding tasks, reducing the risk of worker fatigue and injury. This is particularly important in vehicle manufacturing, where tasks like lifting and assembly can be physically taxing.

- **Flexibility:** Cobots can be easily reprogrammed to perform a wide range of tasks, making them adaptable to different production requirements. This flexibility allows manufacturers to quickly respond to changes in demand or product design.

3.3 Challenges of Cobots

While cobots offer numerous benefits, they also present certain challenges:

- **Safety Concerns:** Although cobots are designed to be safe around humans, there are still potential risks. Manufacturers must ensure that cobots are properly calibrated and equipped with safety features to prevent accidents.

- **Workforce Resistance:** Some workers may resist the integration of cobots due to fears of job displacement or concerns about working with robots. Addressing these concerns requires proper training and communication about how cobots enhance the work process rather than replace human workers.

4. Hands-On Project: Programming a Simple Robot Arm for Assembly Tasks

In this section, we will explore how a simple robot arm can be programmed to perform basic assembly tasks, giving readers a practical understanding of how robots are used in manufacturing.

4.1 Setting Up the Environment

For this project, we will use a simple robotic arm simulator, such as **VEXcode VR** or **Webots**, which allows users to program a virtual robot arm to perform tasks. You can also use physical robot arms such as the **Universal Robots UR3** or **ABB YuMi**, depending on the available hardware.

1. **Install Software:**
   Download and install the simulator or robot programming environment, ensuring it is compatible with your operating system.

2. **Connect the Robot Arm:**
   If using a physical robot arm, connect the robot to the programming environment via USB or network connection. If using a simulator, ensure the robot arm is loaded and ready for programming.

4.2 Programming the Robot Arm

In this tutorial, we will program the robot arm to perform a simple assembly task, such as picking up a part and placing it on a workstation.

1. **Define the Objective:**
    The objective is to pick up a part from a designated location and place it onto a station for further processing.

2. **Write the Code:** We will use Python, a popular programming language in robotics, to control the robot's movements.

python

Copy

```python
import time

from robot_arm import RobotArm


# Initialize robot arm

robot_arm = RobotArm()
```

```python
# Define positions for pick and place

pick_position = (10, 20, 30)

place_position = (40, 50, 60)


# Move to pick position

robot_arm.move_to(pick_position)

robot_arm.pick()


# Move to place position

robot_arm.move_to(place_position)

robot_arm.place()


# Wait for the task to complete

time.sleep(2)


# Return to home position

robot_arm.move_to((0, 0, 0))
```

Explanation of Code:

- ○ The move_to function moves the arm to a specific coordinate in 3D space.

- ○ The pick function activates the gripper to pick up the object.

- ○ The place function places the object onto the workstation.

4.3 Testing the Program

Once the code is written, it is time to test it. Run the program in the simulator or on the physical robot arm, ensuring that the robot follows the defined movements accurately. Observe how the robot picks up the part, moves it to the workstation, and places it correctly.

4.4 Troubleshooting and Refinement

During testing, you may encounter issues such as the robot arm not reaching the correct position or dropping the part. To troubleshoot, check the following:

- **Positioning:** Ensure that the coordinates for the pick and place positions are correct.

- **Timing:** Adjust the timing between movements to ensure the robot has enough time to pick up and place the part.

- **Calibration:** Verify that the robot arm is properly calibrated and that the gripper is functioning correctly.

Conclusion

The integration of AI and robotics in vehicle manufacturing is transforming the industry, enhancing precision, efficiency, and flexibility. By automating assembly lines, manufacturers are able to produce vehicles faster and with greater accuracy. Collaborative robots (cobots) are also playing an increasingly important role in improving workplace ergonomics and productivity. However, while the benefits of robotics and AI are clear, there are still challenges that need to be addressed, such as safety, workforce adaptation, and system integration.

In this chapter, we have explored the profound impact of AI and robotics on vehicle manufacturing, examined the benefits and challenges of automation in assembly lines, and highlighted the role of collaborative robots in improving manufacturing processes. Through the hands-on project, you gained a practical understanding of how robots are programmed for assembly tasks, providing a foundation for more complex robotics applications in manufacturing.

The future of vehicle manufacturing will continue to evolve as AI and robotics advance, and these technologies will remain at the heart of innovation in the automotive industry. By mastering these technologies, developers and manufacturers will be able to create more efficient, safe, and customizable vehicles that meet the demands of tomorrow's consumers.

Chapter 10: Ethics and Regulation in Autonomous Vehicles

Introduction: Navigating the Intersection of Technology, Ethics, and Law

The development of autonomous vehicles (AVs) has raised not only technical questions but also profound ethical and legal challenges. As AVs become more integrated into society, they promise to revolutionize transportation, reduce accidents, and improve efficiency. However, their rise has also sparked debates about the ethics of decision-making, the regulation of emerging technologies, and the legal frameworks necessary to ensure that AVs operate safely and fairly within society.

In this chapter, we will examine the ethical dilemmas AVs face, particularly in critical decision-making scenarios, and discuss how governments and regulatory bodies are stepping in to create guidelines for their development and deployment. We will also explore how different countries regulate autonomous vehicles and predict the future trajectory of AV legislation.

---

1. Ethical Considerations in Autonomous Vehicles

The ethical concerns surrounding autonomous vehicles are multifaceted and complex. One of the primary ethical questions in AV development revolves around how an autonomous vehicle should make decisions, especially in life-threatening situations. These dilemmas are often exemplified by the "trolley problem," a thought experiment that raises significant moral questions about decision-making in the face of unavoidable harm.

1.1 The Trolley Problem: Autonomous Vehicles and Moral Dilemmas

The trolley problem is a well-known ethical thought experiment that presents a moral dilemma in which a person must choose between two actions: one that will lead to harm and one that will prevent greater harm but result in the loss of a life. For example, in its simplest form, the problem involves a runaway trolley heading towards five people tied to a track. The person standing by a lever can divert the trolley onto another track, where it will kill one person but save five. The ethical dilemma is whether to pull the lever and actively cause one death to save five others, or do nothing and allow the trolley to kill five people.

In the context of autonomous vehicles, similar moral questions arise. AVs must be programmed to make decisions in real-time about how to act in critical situations, such as avoiding pedestrians or other vehicles. For instance, an AV may face a situation where it can either swerve and hit a pedestrian or stay on course and collide with another vehicle, potentially causing harm to its passengers. These decisions raise the question: how should the AV be programmed to choose the lesser evil?

- **Ethical Dilemmas:**
  The challenge is not just deciding what the AV should do, but how to program it to handle such situations without violating moral principles or societal values. The decisions must consider human lives, the safety of passengers, and the broader societal implications of the vehicle's behavior.

- **Utilitarianism vs. Deontology:**
  Different ethical frameworks may lead to different decisions in these situations. A **utilitarian** approach would prioritize minimizing harm and maximizing overall well-being, which might involve sacrificing one person to save many others. On the other hand, a **deontological** approach might argue that certain actions are inherently wrong, regardless of the consequences, and thus would oppose sacrificing one person for the greater good.

1.2 Decision-Making Under Uncertainty: Navigating Complex Scenarios

AVs must often make decisions under conditions of uncertainty, where the outcomes of different actions are unclear, and the vehicle's understanding of the environment may be incomplete or imprecise. These situations can include rapidly changing traffic conditions, ambiguous sensor data, or unpredictable behaviors by pedestrians and other drivers.

- **Perception Challenges:**
  AVs rely on sensors and algorithms to perceive their environment, but these systems are not perfect. Issues such as sensor failure, poor weather conditions, or obstacles obscured from view can lead to uncertainty in the vehicle's decision-making process. In these situations, how should the AV balance caution and responsiveness? Should it err on the side of safety, even at the cost of efficiency?

- **Algorithmic Decision-Making:**
  The role of AI and machine learning in AV decision-making adds another layer of complexity. These systems must be trained to handle uncertain and unforeseen situations, learning from vast datasets and simulated scenarios. But there are risks in how these algorithms are programmed—how can we ensure that the data used for training is unbiased and represents a broad range of real-

world conditions? Furthermore, what happens if the algorithm makes a mistake in a high-risk situation? Ensuring that AVs act responsibly in uncertain environments requires addressing both the technical limitations of current technology and the ethical principles behind decision-making.

2. The Role of Governments and Regulatory Bodies in AV Development

As autonomous vehicles move from concept to reality, governments and regulatory bodies around the world are working to establish guidelines and frameworks that ensure AVs operate safely and ethically. The regulatory landscape for AVs is complex, as it involves a wide range of issues, including safety standards, liability, data privacy, and environmental impact.

2.1 The Challenge of Regulation: Balancing Innovation with Safety

Regulating AVs is challenging because the technology is evolving rapidly, and there is no one-size-fits-all approach. Policymakers must balance the need for innovation—allowing for the development and deployment of AV technologies—while ensuring that these technologies do not pose risks to public safety or privacy.

- **Creating Safety Standards:**
  Governments and international organizations must develop safety standards for autonomous vehicles that cover everything from vehicle design and performance to testing and certification. This includes defining what constitutes "safe" driving for AVs and how these systems should respond in various scenarios, from city streets to highways.

- **Liability and Accountability:**
  One of the key legal issues in AV regulation is determining who is responsible if something goes wrong. In traditional vehicles, the driver is liable for accidents, but with AVs, it is unclear whether the responsibility falls on the manufacturer, the software developer, or the vehicle owner. Regulations must establish clear liability frameworks to ensure that victims of AV-related accidents can seek compensation.

2.2 The Role of International Standards and Collaboration

Because AV technology is being developed globally, international collaboration and the establishment of universal standards are crucial. Countries must work together to harmonize regulations and create globally accepted standards for the testing, certification, and operation of autonomous vehicles.

- **International Agreements:**
  International bodies, such as the United Nations Economic Commission for Europe (UNECE), are working to establish standards for AV development and deployment. These standards aim to ensure that AVs meet certain safety criteria and adhere to traffic laws, regardless of where they are manufactured or used.

- **Cross-Border Data Sharing:**
  AVs rely on data sharing between vehicles, infrastructure, and external systems for optimal performance. This raises concerns about data privacy and security, and regulators must create guidelines for how data is collected, stored, and shared across borders.

3. Case Study: How Different Countries Regulate Autonomous Vehicles

Regulation of autonomous vehicles varies significantly across different countries, with each nation adopting unique approaches based on its legal systems, cultural values, and technological capabilities. Let's explore how some leading countries are addressing the regulation of AVs.

3.1 United States: A State-Driven Approach

In the U.S., regulation of autonomous vehicles is primarily handled at the state level, with each state having the ability to develop its own rules and policies regarding AV testing and deployment. The federal government has issued guidelines, but there is no nationwide mandate for AVs yet.

- **Challenges and Innovations:**
  In states like California and Arizona, AV testing is permitted on public roads, with specific requirements for safety drivers and data collection. These states have also implemented frameworks for vehicle safety, insurance, and liability. However, inconsistencies across states

create challenges for manufacturers, as AVs must comply with varying regulations in different regions.

- **Federal Guidelines:**
  The U.S. National Highway Traffic Safety Administration (NHTSA) has developed voluntary guidelines for AV testing, focusing on safety standards, cybersecurity, and data privacy. However, critics argue that federal regulation is necessary to create a unified approach to AVs across the country.

3.2 European Union: Comprehensive Regulation and Harmonization

The European Union (EU) takes a more centralized approach to AV regulation, working to establish harmonized rules across its member states. The EU has issued a series of regulations and directives aimed at ensuring AVs meet high safety and ethical standards.

- **GDPR and Data Protection:**
  One significant issue in the EU's regulatory framework is the General Data Protection Regulation (GDPR), which ensures that data collected by AVs is protected and that users'

privacy rights are respected. This includes ensuring that data generated by AV sensors, such as location and driving patterns, is anonymized and stored securely.

- **Testing and Deployment:**
The EU has set strict requirements for the testing and deployment of AVs, including mandatory reporting of AV-related accidents and a framework for certification. Countries like Germany and the UK have been at the forefront of implementing these regulations, with Germany even passing a law allowing AVs to be tested on public roads under specific conditions.

3.3 China: A Growing Regulatory Framework

China is rapidly becoming a major player in the development of autonomous vehicles. The country has invested heavily in AV technology and is now working to establish a regulatory framework for AV testing and deployment.

- **Government Support and Standards:**
The Chinese government has been proactive in creating a legal framework for AVs, focusing on safety, cybersecurity, and public safety.

Chinese authorities have also focused on creating standardized road maps and traffic rules for AV testing, particularly in smart cities like Beijing and Shanghai.

- **Ethical Considerations:**
  One area where China is actively developing regulations is in addressing ethical concerns related to AV decision-making. The country is focusing on ensuring that AVs meet both public safety standards and ethical considerations, such as minimizing accidents in emergency situations.

---

4. Discussion: The Future of Autonomous Vehicle Legislation

As autonomous vehicles become increasingly prevalent, the regulatory landscape will continue to evolve. Governments, manufacturers, and the public must work together to create frameworks that balance innovation, safety, and ethics. Some key areas where we expect significant development in the future include:

4.1 Global Regulatory Harmonization

As AVs become a global phenomenon, the need for a harmonized regulatory approach will become more pressing. Countries will need to collaborate to create international standards for AV testing, safety, and deployment. This will involve addressing issues related to data privacy, cross-border regulation, and liability in the event of an accident.

4.2 Addressing the Ethics of AI Decision-Making

As autonomous vehicles become more intelligent, they will face increasingly complex ethical decisions. Governments and manufacturers will need to establish clear guidelines for AVs' decision-making processes, particularly in critical situations. These guidelines must balance public safety, fairness, and transparency, ensuring that AVs act in ways that align with societal values.

4.3 The Role of Insurance and Liability in AV Regulation

The rise of autonomous vehicles will undoubtedly change the insurance landscape. As AVs become more common, new models of insurance will be required, especially when it comes to liability in the event of accidents. The regulatory framework must address these concerns, ensuring that victims of accidents involving AVs are compensated fairly.

Conclusion

Ethics and regulation are critical components of autonomous vehicle development. As AVs become an integral part of our transportation system, it is essential that governments, manufacturers, and society at large collaborate to address the ethical, legal, and societal challenges these vehicles present. From moral dilemmas in decision-making to regulatory frameworks for testing and deployment, the future of AVs hinges on our ability to navigate these complex issues. Through careful consideration and regulation, we can ensure that autonomous vehicles contribute to a safer, more efficient, and ethical transportation system.

This chapter has explored the ethical considerations, regulatory challenges, and legal frameworks shaping the development of autonomous vehicles. It has also provided insight into how different countries are regulating AVs and how legislation may evolve in the future. By addressing these challenges head-on, we can ensure that autonomous vehicles are developed in a way that benefits society and operates within the bounds of ethical and legal guidelines.

Chapter 11: Human-Robot Interaction (HRI) in Autonomous Vehicles

Introduction: The Importance of HRI for Autonomous Vehicles in Public Spaces

Human-Robot Interaction (HRI) is an essential component of the autonomous vehicle (AV) ecosystem. While the technical capabilities of AVs—such as navigation, perception, and decision-making—are advancing rapidly, the success of AV deployment in public spaces hinges on effective interaction between AVs and humans. This interaction involves not only the communication between the vehicle and its passengers but also how AVs interact with pedestrians, other drivers, and the broader road ecosystem.

As autonomous vehicles are increasingly integrated into urban environments, the ability for AVs to collaborate and communicate with human road users becomes paramount. Unlike traditional vehicles, which are operated by human drivers, AVs must be able to convey their intentions and understand the intentions of others. This mutual understanding is critical for ensuring safe and efficient operation in complex public spaces, where unpredictable human behaviors and interactions are common.

This chapter explores the critical role of HRI in the development of AVs, addressing the design of systems that facilitate communication and collaboration between AVs and humans. Additionally, we will delve into the challenges of designing these systems, focusing on how to foster human acceptance and trust in autonomous technology. The chapter will conclude with a hands-on project, where we will design a simple human-vehicle interaction model to demonstrate the practical application of these concepts.

1. Designing Systems for Communication and Collaboration Between AVs and Humans

The key to successful HRI in autonomous vehicles lies in designing systems that allow the vehicle to communicate its intentions clearly and effectively to human users, while also enabling it to understand and respond to human behavior.

1.1 The Role of Communication in Human-Robot Interaction

Communication is at the heart of all effective human-robot interactions. In the context of AVs, communication occurs on two levels:

1. **Vehicle-to-Pedestrian Communication:** AVs must communicate their intentions to pedestrians, cyclists, and other road users. For instance, when an AV stops to allow a pedestrian to cross, it must signal its intent to stop, and pedestrians must recognize that the vehicle has stopped for them.

2. **Vehicle-to-Vehicle Communication:** AVs must also communicate with other vehicles on the road. This may involve signaling lane changes,

decelerating, or preparing to stop, especially in high-traffic situations.

The challenge lies in designing intuitive communication methods that are universally understood by all human road users, regardless of their background or familiarity with autonomous technology.

- **Visual Indicators:**
  One of the most common methods for AVs to communicate with humans is through visual indicators, such as lights, displays, or movement cues. For example, many AVs use lights to signal their intentions, such as a green light indicating that the vehicle is ready to proceed or a flashing light indicating that the vehicle is stopping.

- **Auditory Signals:**
  In some scenarios, AVs may use sound signals, such as horns or voice prompts, to communicate with pedestrians or other vehicles. This can be particularly useful in noisy urban environments where visual signals may be less effective.

- **Physical Gestures:**
  AVs can also use physical gestures to communicate, such as turning or slowing down in a manner that is predictable and understandable to humans. Additionally, researchers are exploring the possibility of using robotic arms or other external features to signal the vehicle's intentions in a more obvious and human-like manner.

1.2 The Vehicle's Understanding of Human Behavior

In addition to communicating effectively with humans, AVs must also be capable of understanding and responding to human actions. This requires sophisticated perception systems that can recognize the behavior and intentions of pedestrians, cyclists, and other drivers.

- **Pedestrian Recognition:**
  AVs rely on cameras, lidar, radar, and other sensors to detect pedestrians and understand their movements. By analyzing a pedestrian's position, speed, and trajectory, the vehicle can predict their behavior and adjust its actions accordingly. For example, if a pedestrian steps

into a crosswalk, the AV must recognize their presence and prepare to stop.

- **Driver Behavior Understanding:**
  AVs must also understand the behavior of human drivers. This involves recognizing signals like turn indicators, brake lights, or the general movement patterns of other vehicles. The vehicle must anticipate potential conflicts or opportunities for collaboration, such as yielding the right of way or adjusting speed to maintain a safe distance from other cars.

---

2. Challenges in Designing for Human Acceptance and Trust

For AVs to be widely accepted and successfully integrated into society, they must be able to earn the trust of human road users. This requires addressing several key challenges related to human behavior, perceptions, and trust in autonomous systems.

2.1 Perception of Safety: Building Trust in AV Systems

One of the primary concerns for the public regarding autonomous vehicles is safety. Unlike human drivers,

AVs rely on algorithms and sensors to make decisions, and many people are skeptical about the vehicle's ability to make life-or-death decisions in critical situations. For example, in a complex traffic scenario where a human driver would have to make a split-second decision, can an AV respond as quickly and effectively?

- **Challenge:**
  Humans tend to trust other humans more than machines, especially in high-stakes situations. Autonomous vehicles must be designed to give people confidence that they will make safe decisions, even when faced with uncertainty or emergency situations.

- **Solution Approach:**
  To address these concerns, AV manufacturers are focusing on building transparent systems that can explain the reasoning behind the vehicle's decisions. This might involve providing real-time feedback to passengers about the vehicle's actions or using visual or auditory cues to communicate the vehicle's decisions.

2.2 Predictability and Transparency: Ensuring Clear Interaction Cues

Another challenge in designing AV systems is ensuring that human road users can predict the behavior of autonomous vehicles. Human drivers typically rely on a combination of verbal cues, body language, and other non-verbal signals to understand the intentions of other drivers. For AVs to be effective, they must also exhibit predictable behaviors that can be easily interpreted by human users.

- **Challenge:**
  AVs must make their actions as transparent as possible, signaling to other drivers or pedestrians what they intend to do next. For instance, if an AV intends to stop at a crosswalk, it must give clear and predictable visual or behavioral signals so pedestrians know they are safe to cross.

- **Solution Approach:**
  Designers are exploring methods for increasing predictability, such as programming AVs to perform actions in a way that mimics human behavior. This might involve incorporating cues like decelerating slightly before stopping, or

gradually increasing speed when it's safe to move forward.

2.3 Human Comfort: Reducing Anxiety and Fostering Trust

Trust is not just about safety—it's also about comfort. Human drivers and passengers often feel a sense of anxiety or discomfort when they experience a loss of control. In an AV, passengers cannot directly intervene in the driving process, which can lead to feelings of unease, especially in unfamiliar or complex driving situations.

- **Challenge:**
  Passengers may experience "motion sickness" or anxiety if the AV's driving style is too erratic or unpredictable. AVs must be programmed to provide a smooth and comfortable ride, with gentle acceleration, braking, and steering.

- **Solution Approach:**
  Developers are working to optimize AV driving algorithms for comfort. This includes programming vehicles to respond smoothly to road conditions, traffic patterns, and environmental factors, ensuring that the

vehicle's movements are predictable and comfortable for passengers.

---

3. Project: Designing a Simple Human-Vehicle Interaction Model

In this section, we will walk through a hands-on project to design a simple human-vehicle interaction model. This model will simulate how an autonomous vehicle might communicate with pedestrians and other vehicles in a real-world scenario.

3.1 Defining the Objective

The objective of this project is to design an interaction model where the AV uses visual signals (such as lights or indicators) to communicate with pedestrians and other vehicles. The vehicle will communicate its intentions, such as stopping or accelerating, to ensure safe interaction with human road users.

3.2 Setting Up the Environment

To simulate the interaction model, we will use a virtual environment, such as **Unity3D** or **Webots**, which allows us to create simple simulations of AVs in a 3D space. These platforms provide tools for creating realistic road environments and programming the vehicle's behavior.

- **Step 1: Create the Road Environment**
  Begin by designing a simple road environment with a crosswalk and a pedestrian. Add a vehicle to the simulation and position it at a traffic light.

- **Step 2: Program the Vehicle's Behavior**
  Program the vehicle to detect the presence of pedestrians in the crosswalk. If a pedestrian is detected, the vehicle will stop and activate a visual signal (such as flashing lights) to indicate that it is yielding to the pedestrian.

python

Copy

```python
# Simple Python Code for AV interaction
import time


class AutonomousVehicle:
    def __init__(self, position):
        self.position = position
```

```python
        self.lights_on = False


    def detect_pedestrian(self, pedestrian_position):
        if self.position == pedestrian_position:
            return True
        return False


    def stop_vehicle(self):
        print("Vehicle stopped.")
        self.lights_on = True
        print("Flashing lights to indicate stopping.")


    def move_vehicle(self):
        print("Vehicle moving forward.")
        self.lights_on = False

# Define positions for the vehicle and pedestrian
vehicle = AutonomousVehicle(position=0)
```

```
pedestrian_position = 5


# Simulate pedestrian detection and vehicle behavior

if vehicle.detect_pedestrian(pedestrian_position):

    vehicle.stop_vehicle()

else:

    vehicle.move_vehicle()


time.sleep(2)
```

3.3 Testing and Refining the Model

Once the basic interaction is programmed, test the model by simulating different scenarios. For instance, test how the vehicle behaves when pedestrians approach, whether it yields correctly, and if it communicates its intentions clearly.

3.4 Evaluating Human Responses

Next, consider how a human observer might respond to the AV's communication signals. Are the signals clear and understandable? Would a pedestrian feel confident crossing the street based on the AV's behavior? Evaluate the system's effectiveness by adjusting the visual cues and testing different driving scenarios.

Conclusion

Human-Robot Interaction is a critical aspect of autonomous vehicle development. For AVs to integrate seamlessly into public spaces, they must communicate clearly with human road users, understand human behavior, and foster trust. This chapter has explored the various dimensions of HRI in autonomous vehicles, from designing communication systems to addressing the challenges of human acceptance and comfort.

Through the hands-on project, we demonstrated how a simple human-vehicle interaction model can be designed to facilitate communication and collaboration between AVs and pedestrians. By addressing the key challenges of safety, predictability, and comfort, we can develop AV systems that earn public trust and create a safer, more efficient transportation system for the future.

As AV technology continues to evolve, HRI will remain a fundamental focus of development, ensuring that autonomous vehicles can coexist with human road users in a way that is both safe and intuitive. This chapter provides the foundation for understanding the importance of HRI in AVs and offers practical insights for future developments in this area.

Chapter 12: The Future of Autonomous Mobility: From Cars to Smart Cities

Introduction: The Shift Towards Autonomous Mobility and Smart Cities

Autonomous mobility, spearheaded by the development of autonomous vehicles (AVs), promises to reshape how we think about transportation. While much of the current conversation around AVs focuses on personal vehicles, their integration into the broader fabric of smart cities is poised to revolutionize urban living. The concept of a smart city—where digital technologies and data-driven systems optimize everything from energy usage to public services—naturally aligns with the capabilities of AVs, which rely on data, connectivity, and advanced algorithms to operate efficiently.

The integration of AVs into urban infrastructure has the potential to enhance mobility, reduce traffic congestion, improve safety, and create a more sustainable and efficient transportation ecosystem. This chapter will explore how AVs fit into the vision of smart cities, the role of artificial intelligence (AI) in traffic management and Mobility as a Service (MaaS), and how AVs will reshape transportation networks and urban planning in the coming decades. We will also examine a real-world case study of a city implementing autonomous shuttle systems to understand the practical steps being taken toward this future.

1. The Integration of Autonomous Vehicles in Smart Cities

A smart city uses technology to enhance the quality of life for its residents, optimize resource usage, and improve urban services. AVs fit seamlessly into this vision, offering the promise of more efficient, safer, and environmentally friendly transportation. By incorporating AVs into smart city infrastructure, urban planners can address many of the current challenges cities face, including traffic congestion, pollution, and inefficiencies in public transport systems.

1.1 Smart Cities and AVs: A Symbiotic Relationship

The relationship between AVs and smart cities is symbiotic. While AVs can optimize transportation, smart city infrastructure provides the framework that enables AVs to operate effectively. Key components of this infrastructure include:

- **IoT and Sensor Networks:** Smart cities rely heavily on Internet of Things (IoT) devices and sensors to monitor traffic patterns, air quality, and infrastructure usage. These sensors collect data that can be used by AVs to make real-time decisions, such as adjusting speed based on traffic conditions or detecting obstacles in the road ahead.

- **Vehicle-to-Everything (V2X) Communication:** AVs communicate with each other, traffic lights, pedestrians, and even infrastructure like smart roads to ensure smooth and safe operations. In smart cities, V2X communication is crucial for enabling these interactions and ensuring that AVs can navigate urban environments safely and efficiently.

- **Centralized Data Management:** In smart cities, vast amounts of data are collected from sensors, AVs, and other sources. This data can be used to optimize traffic flow, manage public services, and improve overall urban planning. AI and machine learning models process this data to predict traffic patterns, adjust signals in real-time, and manage demand for transportation services.

1.2 AVs in the Context of Urban Infrastructure

For AVs to integrate seamlessly into smart cities, urban infrastructure must be adapted to support their needs. This includes everything from smart traffic lights and road markings to dedicated lanes for AVs. Some of the key considerations include:

- **Infrastructure Upgrades:** Roads and intersections may need to be redesigned or retrofitted to accommodate AVs. This could involve adding features like dedicated AV lanes, sensors embedded in the road, and smart traffic lights that communicate directly with AVs to optimize traffic flow.

- **Data-Driven Urban Planning:** Urban planners will need to use data collected from AVs and IoT devices to design cities that maximize efficiency and safety. This may involve designing streetscapes that prioritize pedestrians, cyclists, and AVs, creating hubs for shared autonomous transport, and integrating AVs into broader mobility systems.

2. The Role of AI in Traffic Management and Mobility as a Service (MaaS)

AI plays a pivotal role in the management of smart cities and the integration of AVs into urban transportation systems. From optimizing traffic flow to enabling the concept of Mobility as a Service (MaaS), AI can significantly enhance the efficiency of urban transportation.

2.1 AI in Traffic Management

Traffic congestion is one of the most pressing issues faced by cities today. AI can help alleviate congestion by improving traffic flow, reducing bottlenecks, and making real-time adjustments based on traffic conditions. Some of the ways AI can be used in traffic management include:

- **Predictive Traffic Flow:** AI models can analyze real-time traffic data to predict congestion and adjust traffic signals accordingly. For example, AI can use data from sensors, cameras, and GPS to predict where traffic will build up and adjust light timings to minimize delays.

- **Adaptive Traffic Signals:** AI-powered traffic signals can change in real-time based on traffic conditions. For instance, if an AV is approaching an intersection, the signal could automatically adjust to prioritize the vehicle's passage, improving efficiency and reducing wait times.

- **Coordinated AV Movement:** In a smart city, AI can coordinate the movement of AVs to optimize traffic flow. By communicating with other vehicles and traffic management systems, AVs can adjust their speed, trajectory, and route to minimize congestion, improve safety, and enhance the overall efficiency of the transportation network.

2.2 Mobility as a Service (MaaS)

MaaS is a concept that integrates various forms of transportation—such as buses, trains, bicycles, and shared AVs—into a single, unified service that users can access via a mobile app or platform. AI plays a crucial role in enabling MaaS by providing real-time data analysis, route optimization, and seamless integration of different transportation modes.

- **Route Optimization:** AI can analyze traffic patterns, weather conditions, and user preferences to suggest the fastest, most efficient route, whether the user is driving their own vehicle or using a shared AV. For instance, AI can determine whether it's better for a user to take a shared AV, a bus, or a bike based on current conditions and personal preferences.

- **Seamless Integration of Transportation Modes:** MaaS platforms powered by AI can integrate multiple modes of transport, providing users with a one-stop solution for all their travel needs. For example, a user could plan a trip that involves taking a shared autonomous vehicle to a subway station, followed by a train ride to their destination, all within one seamless platform.

- **Dynamic Pricing:** AI can also be used to implement dynamic pricing in MaaS systems. By analyzing demand, traffic conditions, and availability, AI can adjust prices in real-time to ensure that the system operates efficiently while also encouraging sustainable travel behaviors.

---

3. How AVs Will Change Transportation Networks and Urban Planning

The widespread adoption of AVs will significantly transform urban transportation networks and the way cities are planned and structured. AVs will reduce the need for personal vehicle ownership, optimize public transportation systems, and introduce new paradigms in urban mobility.

3.1 The Impact on Transportation Networks

- **Reduced Traffic Congestion:** With AVs communicating and coordinating with one another, transportation networks will become more efficient. This could lead to reduced traffic congestion, as AVs will be able to adjust their routes and speeds to avoid bottlenecks. Additionally, AVs will enable more efficient use of road space, as they can drive more closely together without compromising safety.

- **Optimization of Public Transport:** AVs could become a key component of public transportation systems, particularly in areas with low population density. Autonomous buses, shuttles, and ride-sharing services could provide flexible, on-demand transportation options, reducing the need for traditional bus routes and reducing congestion in city centers.

- **Safety Improvements:** The integration of AVs into urban transportation systems is expected to reduce traffic accidents. By removing human error from driving, AVs can prevent the majority of accidents caused by distractions, fatigue, or impaired driving. Furthermore, AI-driven traffic management systems can help reduce accidents by optimizing the flow of traffic and preventing congestion.

3.2 Urban Planning in the Age of AVs

Urban planning will undergo a transformation as AVs become more prevalent. The design of cities will need to evolve to accommodate the new realities of autonomous mobility, with changes in infrastructure, land use, and transportation networks.

- **Reimagining Parking and Road Infrastructure:** With the rise of AVs, traditional parking structures may become obsolete, as vehicles could drop passengers off at their destination and then park themselves remotely in more efficient, centralized locations. This could free up valuable urban space, which could be repurposed for parks, commercial spaces, or residential developments.

- **Redesigning Streetscapes:** As AVs become more common, streets may be redesigned to prioritize pedestrians, cyclists, and shared AVs.

For example, urban planners may design more pedestrian-friendly zones and dedicate specific lanes for AVs, further improving safety and efficiency in urban areas.

- **Increased Focus on Sustainability:** AVs are expected to reduce carbon emissions by optimizing traffic flow and promoting shared, electric transportation options. In smart cities, this could lead to reduced reliance on fossil-fuel-powered vehicles and a shift toward electric, autonomous public transport options.

4. Case Study: A City Implementing Autonomous Shuttle Systems

To better understand how autonomous vehicles are already being integrated into smart city infrastructure, we will examine a case study of a city that has implemented autonomous shuttle systems.

4.1 City Overview: San Francisco, California

San Francisco is one of the leading cities in the United States when it comes to testing and deploying autonomous vehicles. The city has partnered with several companies to introduce autonomous shuttle services as part of its broader smart city initiatives.

- **Objective:**
  The primary goal of the autonomous shuttle project is to provide a sustainable, on-demand public transportation option that reduces congestion, lowers carbon emissions, and improves accessibility for residents. The shuttle systems are designed to integrate seamlessly into the city's existing public transportation infrastructure, providing first-mile/last-mile connectivity.

4.2 Implementation and Operation of Autonomous Shuttles

- **Technology Used:**
  The shuttles are equipped with a variety of sensors, including lidar, cameras, and radar, to navigate through the city streets and communicate with other vehicles and infrastructure. The vehicles are also equipped with AI-driven algorithms that allow them to adapt to real-time traffic conditions and pedestrian movements.

- **User Experience:**
  Riders can hail autonomous shuttles using a mobile app, which allows them to book rides in real-time. The shuttles operate on fixed routes but are flexible enough to adjust based on demand and traffic conditions.

- **Challenges Faced:**
  One of the primary challenges faced by the city in implementing autonomous shuttles has been ensuring the safety of both passengers and pedestrians. To address this, the shuttles are operated with a safety driver onboard, ready to intervene in case of an emergency. However, the city is working toward fully autonomous operation without the need for human oversight.

4.3 Results and Impact

- **Improved Mobility:**
  The autonomous shuttle system has provided a convenient and efficient transportation option for residents, particularly in areas that are underserved by traditional public transportation.

- **Traffic and Congestion Reduction:**
  Early data suggests that the introduction of autonomous shuttles has helped reduce congestion by providing an alternative to personal car ownership, particularly in densely populated urban areas.

- **Future Plans:**
  As the technology matures, the city plans to expand the shuttle system to other neighborhoods and integrate it with other forms of transportation, such as electric bikes and traditional buses, to create a seamless, multimodal mobility network.

5. The Future of Autonomous Mobility and Smart Cities

The future of autonomous mobility is closely tied to the evolution of smart cities. As AVs become a more prominent part of urban transportation networks, they will contribute to the development of more efficient, sustainable, and livable cities. However, realizing this future will require overcoming technical, regulatory, and social challenges.

5.1 Ongoing Innovation in AV and Smart City Technologies

- **AI and Data Integration:**
  As AI technologies evolve, they will enable even greater integration between AVs and the smart city infrastructure. Real-time data analysis, machine learning models, and cloud computing will allow AVs to interact with their environment in increasingly sophisticated ways.

- **Sustainability and Environmental Impact:**
  Autonomous mobility has the potential to reduce greenhouse gas emissions by optimizing transportation routes, promoting shared mobility, and transitioning to electric vehicles. Cities will need to prioritize sustainability in their AV integration strategies.

5.2 The Role of Public-Private Partnerships

Successful integration of AVs into smart cities will require collaboration between government entities, private companies, and research institutions. Public-private partnerships will be key in ensuring that the necessary infrastructure, regulations, and technological advancements are in place to support autonomous mobility.

Conclusion

The integration of autonomous vehicles into smart cities marks the beginning of a new era in urban mobility. AVs, powered by AI and connected infrastructure, have the potential to revolutionize transportation networks, improve safety, reduce congestion, and create more sustainable and efficient cities. By examining how AVs will reshape transportation networks, urban planning, and mobility as a service (MaaS), this chapter has provided a comprehensive understanding of the transformative impact of autonomous mobility.

Through real-world case studies and exploration of future technologies, we can see that autonomous vehicles will not only change how we travel but also how we live in cities. As technology, regulations, and societal acceptance evolve, the future of autonomous mobility will continue to shape the cities of tomorrow, offering a vision of a smarter, more connected world.

Chapter 13: AI in Autonomous Vehicle Safety and Security

Introduction: The Critical Role of Safety and Security in Autonomous Vehicles

Autonomous vehicles (AVs) hold the potential to revolutionize transportation, improving efficiency, safety, and reducing traffic-related fatalities. However, the introduction of AVs into public roads brings with it significant challenges in ensuring both safety and security. Unlike human-driven vehicles, AVs rely on artificial intelligence (AI), sensors, and algorithms to navigate their environment and make decisions in real-time. While these systems are designed to enhance safety, they also introduce new risks, particularly in the areas of cybersecurity.

This chapter will explore how AI plays a critical role in ensuring the safety of autonomous vehicles, focusing on accident prevention, hazard detection, and cybersecurity. We will also examine the vulnerabilities that AVs face, including hacking and system failures, and discuss how AI can be used to address these concerns. Additionally, we will present a hands-on project that demonstrates the development of a basic hazard detection system, offering readers a practical introduction to the safety features of AVs.

---

1. Cybersecurity Risks in Autonomous Vehicles

As autonomous vehicles become increasingly reliant on AI and connected systems, the importance of cybersecurity grows exponentially. AVs are essentially mobile computers on wheels, constantly collecting, processing, and transmitting vast amounts of data. This makes them vulnerable to cyberattacks, which could compromise their safety, privacy, and functionality.

1.1 Vulnerabilities in AV Systems

AVs are equipped with a wide range of sensors, cameras, GPS systems, and communication protocols to navigate and interact with the environment. These components create multiple entry points for cyberattacks. Key vulnerabilities in AVs include:

- **Sensor Hijacking:**
  AVs rely on sensors such as lidar, radar, cameras, and ultrasonic sensors to perceive their environment. If these sensors are tampered with or spoofed, an attacker could trick the vehicle into making incorrect decisions, such as failing to detect obstacles or misjudging the speed of surrounding vehicles.

- **Vehicle-to-Everything (V2X) Communication Attacks:**
  V2X communication allows AVs to interact with other vehicles, traffic signals, and infrastructure. While this enhances safety and efficiency, it also opens the door to potential attacks. For example, a hacker could manipulate signals sent to or from the vehicle,

potentially causing it to make unsafe maneuvers or even crash.

- **Over-the-Air (OTA) Software Updates:**
Many AV manufacturers use over-the-air updates to patch software vulnerabilities, update navigation maps, or improve the vehicle's AI capabilities. While OTA updates are convenient and efficient, they can also be a potential attack vector. If an attacker intercepts or manipulates these updates, they could introduce malicious code into the vehicle's system.

- **Remote Control and Hacking:**
AVs are typically connected to the cloud, allowing for remote diagnostics and troubleshooting. However, this connection also presents the risk of hacking. Malicious actors could potentially gain control of the vehicle remotely, overriding safety features, manipulating controls, or stealing sensitive data.

1.2 The Importance of Cybersecurity in AV Development

Ensuring that AVs are secure from cyber threats is critical not only for the protection of the vehicle's occupants but also for public safety. Cybersecurity protocols must be integrated into every aspect of AV design, from hardware and software development to communication protocols and data storage.

- **Encryption and Authentication:**
  To protect data transmitted between AVs and external systems (such as infrastructure, traffic signals, or other vehicles), strong encryption techniques are essential. Additionally, robust authentication measures must be implemented to ensure that only authorized entities can access and control the vehicle's systems.

- **Redundancy and Fail-Safe Mechanisms:**
  AV systems should be designed with redundancy and fail-safe mechanisms in place to prevent single points of failure. For example, if one sensor is compromised or fails, the system should automatically switch to a backup sensor to maintain functionality.

- **Security Testing and Audits:**
  Regular security testing, vulnerability assessments, and audits should be conducted to identify potential weaknesses in AV systems. This proactive approach to cybersecurity helps to prevent breaches and ensures that the vehicle remains secure over time.

---

2. The Role of AI in Ensuring Safety and Mitigating Accidents

One of the primary goals of autonomous vehicles is to reduce accidents caused by human error, which accounts for a significant portion of traffic-related fatalities. AI plays a crucial role in improving vehicle safety by enhancing decision-making capabilities and providing real-time analysis of the vehicle's environment. Through advanced algorithms, machine learning, and sensor fusion, AI enables AVs to identify and respond to potential hazards more effectively than human drivers.

2.1 AI-Powered Decision Making in AVs

AI enables AVs to process and analyze data from multiple sensors, making decisions based on the vehicle's environment. The AI system must be able to make split-second decisions in complex and dynamic environments, such as city streets or highway traffic. Some key areas where AI enhances safety include:

- **Object Detection and Classification:** Using deep learning techniques, AVs can recognize and classify objects such as pedestrians, other vehicles, cyclists, and road obstacles. AI algorithms are trained on large datasets to identify these objects in various conditions, such as low-light environments or inclement weather.

- **Predictive Decision Making:** AI can predict the behavior of other road users by analyzing historical data and real-time movements. For example, the system can anticipate a pedestrian's intention to cross the street or predict that a vehicle in an adjacent lane is about to change lanes. These predictions allow the AV to take proactive measures, such as slowing down or changing lanes, to avoid potential collisions.

- **Path Planning and Collision Avoidance:** AI plays a critical role in calculating the optimal path for the vehicle to follow while avoiding obstacles and staying within traffic laws. In emergency situations, AI can quickly compute alternative routes to avoid collisions and minimize risk.

- **Driver Assistance and Emergency Maneuvers:**
  While fully autonomous vehicles are designed to drive without human intervention, many AV systems still include driver assistance features, such as emergency braking and lane-keeping assist. AI helps make real-time decisions about when these systems should be activated to prevent accidents.

2.2 Mitigating Accidents Through AI and Sensor Fusion

One of the primary ways that AI contributes to AV safety is through sensor fusion—the integration of data from multiple sensors to create a comprehensive understanding of the environment. By combining data from radar, lidar, cameras, and ultrasonic sensors, AI can provide a more accurate and reliable assessment of the surroundings.

- **Enhanced Detection and Tracking:**
  Sensor fusion allows AVs to track objects in the environment more accurately. For example, radar and lidar can detect obstacles at longer ranges, while cameras provide high-resolution images to identify specific objects, such as pedestrians or traffic signs. The AI system can then combine this information to make informed decisions about the vehicle's next action.

- **Handling Adverse Conditions:**
  In challenging conditions, such as fog, rain, or snow, AI can leverage sensor fusion to compensate for the limitations of individual sensors. For example, while cameras may struggle in low-light environments, lidar and radar can provide more reliable data, enabling the AV to navigate safely despite adverse conditions.

2.3 Continuous Learning and Improvement

AI systems in AVs are not static—they continuously learn and improve through experience. As an AV operates in the real world, it collects data from every interaction with its environment, which is then used to refine and enhance its decision-making algorithms. This process, known as reinforcement learning, enables AVs to adapt to new and unforeseen scenarios.

- **Learning from Mistakes:**
  If an AV makes a mistake, such as failing to recognize an obstacle in its path, the system can learn from this experience and update its algorithms to avoid similar mistakes in the future. This continuous feedback loop helps to improve the vehicle's safety over time.

- **Sharing Data for Collective Improvement:**
  Autonomous vehicles are connected to cloud-based systems that allow them to share data with other vehicles and infrastructure. By aggregating data from a fleet of AVs, manufacturers can identify patterns, improve safety features, and ensure that all vehicles benefit from shared learning.

3. How AVs Detect and React to Potential Hazards

Detecting and responding to potential hazards is a fundamental aspect of autonomous vehicle safety. AVs must be capable of recognizing hazards such as pedestrians, cyclists, other vehicles, road debris, or sudden obstacles, and taking appropriate action to mitigate risk.

3.1 Hazard Detection Algorithms

AI-powered hazard detection systems use a combination of machine learning, sensor data, and pattern recognition to identify potential threats. Some of the key methods used by AVs for hazard detection include:

- **Convolutional Neural Networks (CNNs):** CNNs are a type of deep learning algorithm used for image and video recognition. They are particularly effective for detecting objects in visual data from cameras. CNNs can be trained to recognize various hazards, such as pedestrians, cyclists, or animals, by analyzing the pixels in camera images.

- **Radar and Lidar Data Processing:**
  Radar and lidar provide accurate 3D spatial data, allowing AVs to detect objects at a distance, even in low-visibility conditions. AI algorithms process this data to determine the size, shape, and location of objects, helping the vehicle identify potential hazards such as vehicles ahead, stopped traffic, or road obstacles.

- **Fusion of Multiple Sensors:**
  Sensor fusion techniques combine the data from cameras, lidar, radar, and other sensors to create a comprehensive view of the environment. This multi-sensor approach allows AVs to detect hazards more reliably and respond in a timely manner.

3.2 Reacting to Hazards: Autonomous Decision-Making

Once a hazard is detected, the AV must react in real-time to mitigate the risk of an accident. AI systems use predictive models and decision-making algorithms to determine the best course of action.

- **Emergency Braking:**
  If a collision is imminent, the AV may

automatically apply the brakes to avoid or reduce the impact. AI systems calculate the stopping distance and determine if braking is sufficient to avoid the collision, taking into account the vehicle's speed and the distance to the hazard.

- **Avoidance Maneuvers:**
  In some situations, the best course of action may not be to stop but to steer around the obstacle. AI systems calculate the optimal path to avoid the hazard while maintaining vehicle stability and safety. This may involve swerving or changing lanes to avoid an obstruction, such as a pedestrian or another vehicle.

- **Collision Prediction:**
  AVs use AI to predict potential collisions based on the movement of surrounding objects. By analyzing the speed, direction, and trajectory of other vehicles and pedestrians, AI can anticipate when a collision might occur and take proactive measures to avoid it.

4. Hands-On: Building a Basic Hazard Detection System

Now that we have discussed the theoretical aspects of hazard detection, let's explore how to build a basic hazard detection system using AI and machine learning. For this project, we will use a Python-based framework and a simple dataset of images and lidar data to detect and classify hazards.

4.1 Setting Up the Development Environment

Before we start coding, make sure you have the necessary tools installed:

1. Python 3.x

2. OpenCV for image processing

3. TensorFlow or PyTorch for machine learning

4. A simple dataset of images with labeled hazards (e.g., pedestrians, vehicles, etc.)

4.2 Data Preprocessing

The first step is to load and preprocess the dataset. This involves resizing images, normalizing pixel values, and splitting the data into training and testing sets.

python

Copy

```python
import cv2

import numpy as np

from sklearn.model_selection import train_test_split


# Load images and labels

images = []  # List of image paths

labels = []  # List of corresponding labels (1 for hazard, 0 for no hazard)


for image_path in images:

    image = cv2.imread(image_path)

    image_resized = cv2.resize(image, (224, 224))  # Resize to match input dimensions of the model

    images.append(image_resized)

    labels.append(label_for_this_image)


# Normalize the pixel values
```

```python
images = np.array(images) / 255.0

labels = np.array(labels)
```

```python
# Split the dataset into training and testing sets

X_train, X_test, y_train, y_test = train_test_split(images, labels, test_size=0.2)
```

4.3 Building the Model

Next, we will use a convolutional neural network (CNN) to classify hazards in the images. The CNN will learn to identify features in the images that indicate the presence of a hazard, such as a pedestrian or vehicle.

python

Copy

```python
import tensorflow as tf

from tensorflow.keras.models import Sequential

from tensorflow.keras.layers import Conv2D, MaxPooling2D, Flatten, Dense


# Build the CNN model
```

```python
model = Sequential([

    Conv2D(32, (3, 3), activation='relu',
input_shape=(224, 224, 3)),

    MaxPooling2D(pool_size=(2, 2)),

    Conv2D(64, (3, 3), activation='relu'),

    MaxPooling2D(pool_size=(2, 2)),

    Flatten(),

    Dense(128, activation='relu'),

    Dense(1, activation='sigmoid')  # Binary
classification: hazard (1) or no hazard (0)

])


model.compile(optimizer='adam',
loss='binary_crossentropy', metrics=['accuracy'])


# Train the model

model.fit(X_train, y_train, epochs=10, batch_size=32,
validation_data=(X_test, y_test))
```

4.4 Evaluating the Model

After training the model, we evaluate its performance on the test set to determine how well it can detect hazards in unseen images.

python

Copy

```python
# Evaluate the model on the test data
test_loss, test_accuracy = model.evaluate(X_test, y_test)
print(f'Test Accuracy: {test_accuracy * 100:.2f}%')
```

4.5 Using the Model for Hazard Detection

Finally, we can use the trained model to predict whether an image contains a hazard. For this, we load a new image and use the model to make a prediction.

python

Copy

```python
# Load a new image for prediction
new_image = cv2.imread('new_image.jpg')
new_image_resized = cv2.resize(new_image, (224, 224)) / 255.0
```

```
prediction =
model.predict(np.expand_dims(new_image_resized,
axis=0))


if prediction >= 0.5:

    print('Hazard detected!')

else:

    print('No hazard detected.')
```

Conclusion

AI plays a central role in ensuring the safety and security of autonomous vehicles. From detecting hazards and mitigating accidents to protecting AVs from cybersecurity risks, AI is fundamental to the successful deployment of autonomous vehicles. By leveraging machine learning, sensor fusion, and advanced algorithms, AVs can anticipate and respond to potential threats in real-time, making driving safer for everyone on the road.

This chapter has explored how AI ensures the safety and security of AVs, discussed the importance of cybersecurity, and provided a hands-on project for building a basic hazard detection system. As AV technology continues to evolve, it will be essential for developers to continually enhance safety features, integrate robust security measures, and ensure that AI systems are trained to handle increasingly complex driving environments.

With these advancements, AVs have the potential to reduce traffic accidents, prevent fatalities, and provide a safer, more secure transportation system for the future.

Chapter 14: Building an Autonomous Vehicle: A Hands-On Project

Introduction: The Road to Autonomous Vehicle Development

Building an autonomous vehicle (AV) from the ground up is a complex and exciting challenge that requires knowledge of robotics, AI, software engineering, and hardware integration. In this chapter, we will walk through the process of building a simple autonomous car using the Robot Operating System (ROS), a popular open-source framework for robot development.

By the end of this chapter, you will have developed a basic autonomous vehicle capable of navigating an environment using sensors, processing data with AI models, and responding to obstacles or dynamic changes in its environment. This hands-on project will guide you through the essential components of AV development, focusing on integrating software and hardware to create a functional autonomous vehicle.

1. Overview of Building a Simple Autonomous Car Using ROS

The Robot Operating System (ROS) is an open-source framework that provides tools and libraries to help developers create complex robotic systems. ROS is widely used in robotics research and development, making it an excellent choice for building autonomous vehicles. It offers libraries for sensor integration, path planning, motion control, and more.

ROS is composed of multiple components that allow you to simulate, test, and deploy autonomous vehicles. These include:

- **ROS Nodes:** A ROS node is a process that performs a specific task, such as reading sensor data or controlling a motor.

- **ROS Topics:** A communication system where nodes can send and receive messages. For example, a sensor node can publish data on a topic, and a control node can subscribe to it to make decisions.

- **ROS Packages:** These are bundles of nodes and other resources used to implement a specific functionality, such as controlling the vehicle's motors or processing lidar data.

- **Gazebo Simulation:** A powerful tool for simulating robots and environments, Gazebo can be used to simulate the movement and environment of the autonomous vehicle before physical testing.

In this project, we will combine these elements to build a simple autonomous car. The vehicle will use sensors like lidar, cameras, and ultrasonic sensors for obstacle detection, and AI models for decision-making and navigation.

2. Setting Up Sensors and AI Models for an Autonomous Vehicle

Before diving into the code and testing, it's important to set up the right sensors and AI models that will enable the vehicle to perceive its environment and make intelligent decisions.

2.1 Choosing the Right Sensors for Autonomous Vehicles

The core functionality of any autonomous vehicle relies heavily on its sensors. These sensors provide the vehicle with the necessary data to understand its environment, detect obstacles, and navigate safely. Below are the primary sensors we'll use for our project:

- **Lidar:** Light Detection and Ranging (Lidar) sensors provide detailed, 360-degree 3D maps of the vehicle's environment. They are essential for precise obstacle detection and navigation. We will simulate lidar data within ROS using a virtual sensor or use a physical lidar for the vehicle if available.

- **Cameras:** Cameras provide visual data that can be processed using image recognition models.

In our autonomous car, cameras will assist in detecting lane markings, road signs, and other dynamic objects. We will use OpenCV for basic image processing.

- **Ultrasonic Sensors:** These sensors are commonly used for short-range object detection, especially for tasks like parking or maneuvering in tight spaces. Ultrasonic sensors will help detect objects in close proximity to the car.

- **IMU (Inertial Measurement Unit):** The IMU provides data about the car's orientation, acceleration, and velocity. This information is crucial for precise motion control and localization in the environment.

2.2 Setting Up ROS for Sensor Integration

With the hardware sensors chosen, it's time to integrate them into ROS. ROS has built-in drivers for many popular sensor types, so we can easily interface with them.

1. **Install ROS:**
   First, we need to install ROS on your system. The steps vary depending on the version and

operating system, but the most common installation method is via the ROS website's instructions or using package managers like apt for Ubuntu.

2. **Configure Sensors in ROS:**

   o **Lidar:** If you're using a simulated lidar sensor (such as the hokuyo sensor), configure it to publish laser scan data to a ROS topic. If you're using a physical lidar, you'll need to install the appropriate drivers and configure the hardware interface in ROS.

Example: A simple lidar configuration in ROS:

xml

Copy

```xml
<launch>
 <node pkg="urg_node" type="urg_node" name="urg_node" />
</launch>
```

- o **Camera:** To interface a camera with ROS, use the usb_cam package to interface with a webcam or any USB camera.

Example: Camera launch configuration:

xml

Copy

```
<launch>
  <node pkg="usb_cam" type="usb_cam_node" name="usb_cam" />
</launch>
```

- o **Ultrasonic Sensors:** The ultrasonic package in ROS can be used to interface ultrasonic sensors. You can connect the sensor data to a topic for further processing.

---

3. Developing the AI Models for Navigation and Decision Making

AI plays a critical role in the autonomy of AVs, particularly in decision-making, navigation, and path planning. In our project, we will focus on simple AI models for decision-making and obstacle avoidance, which will form the backbone of our vehicle's navigation.

3.1 Path Planning and Motion Control

Path planning algorithms are essential for autonomous vehicles to navigate their environment efficiently and safely. For a simple autonomous vehicle, we'll use a basic *A (A-star) algorithm** for path planning. This algorithm calculates the shortest path from a starting point to a destination, considering obstacles along the way.

- *A Path Planning Algorithm:** The A* algorithm combines features of Dijkstra's Algorithm and Greedy Best-First Search to efficiently find the optimal path. It uses a heuristic to estimate the cost from the current position to the destination.

Example (Python pseudo-code for A*):

python

Copy

```python
def a_star(start, goal):
    open_list = [start]
```

```
closed_list = []

while open_list:

    current_node = get_lowest_f_node(open_list)

    if current_node == goal:

        return reconstruct_path(current_node)

    open_list.remove(current_node)

    closed_list.append(current_node)

    for neighbor in get_neighbors(current_node):

        if neighbor not in closed_list:

            open_list.append(neighbor)
```

3.2 Obstacle Detection and Avoidance

Obstacle detection is a key part of an autonomous vehicle's safety system. In our case, we will implement a basic obstacle avoidance system that uses lidar and ultrasonic sensors. The system will constantly monitor the environment and adjust the vehicle's path in real-time to avoid collisions.

- **Obstacle Detection Algorithm:** Using data from the lidar and ultrasonic sensors, we can detect obstacles within a certain radius. If an obstacle is detected, the vehicle will adjust its direction or stop.

Example (ROS with lidar data):

python

Copy

```python
def obstacle_detection(lidar_data):
    for distance in lidar_data:
        if distance < threshold:
            return True  # Obstacle detected
    return False
```

3.3 Integrating AI Models into ROS Nodes

Once we have the AI models for path planning and obstacle detection, we need to integrate them into ROS nodes. A ROS node is a process that runs a specific part of the system, and it communicates with other nodes via topics.

- **Path Planning Node:**
  This node will take the current position and destination of the vehicle, calculate the optimal path using the A* algorithm, and publish the

planned path to a topic that the vehicle's control system will subscribe to.

- **Obstacle Avoidance Node:**
  This node will process sensor data (lidar, ultrasonic) to detect obstacles in real-time and adjust the vehicle's trajectory to avoid collisions.

4. Testing and Iterating on Vehicle Performance

With the sensors and AI models in place, it's time to test the vehicle's performance and iterate on the design.

4.1 Simulating the Autonomous Vehicle in ROS with Gazebo

Before testing the physical vehicle, we will simulate the autonomous car in a virtual environment using **Gazebo**, which integrates seamlessly with ROS. This allows us to test the vehicle's performance, adjust its behavior, and debug issues in a controlled environment.

- **Creating the Simulation Environment:** Using Gazebo, we can create a 3D simulation of a road environment with obstacles, road signs, and other vehicles. This environment can be used to test the vehicle's sensors, AI models, and motion control system.

- **Testing Obstacle Detection:** During simulation, test the vehicle's ability to detect obstacles. Observe whether the vehicle stops or reroutes successfully when an obstacle is detected in its path.

- **Path Planning Validation:** In the simulation, set a destination and evaluate how well the path planning algorithm navigates the vehicle to its target. Adjust parameters such as the heuristic function or obstacle avoidance algorithm to improve the performance.

4.2 Physical Testing and Iteration

Once the system works well in simulation, it's time to test the autonomous vehicle in the real world. This involves integrating the sensors and AI models into a physical robot or vehicle platform and testing its performance in a controlled, safe environment.

- **Controlled Environment Testing:**
  Start by testing the vehicle in a controlled environment such as a parking lot or test track. Begin with basic tasks such as navigating straight lines, turning, and avoiding stationary obstacles.

- **Iterative Improvements:**
  Based on the testing results, identify areas where the vehicle's performance can be improved. This could involve refining the path planning algorithm, improving obstacle detection accuracy, or adjusting the vehicle's speed and control.

5. Conclusion

Building an autonomous vehicle using ROS is a complex but rewarding process that involves integrating sensors, AI models, and motion control algorithms to create a system that can navigate autonomously. This chapter provided a comprehensive guide to building a basic autonomous car, from setting up sensors and developing AI models to testing and iterating on vehicle performance.

By following the steps in this chapter, you now have a functional autonomous vehicle capable of path planning, obstacle detection, and basic navigation. The hands-on project offered in this chapter provides a solid foundation for those interested in pursuing more advanced autonomous vehicle development, from adding more sensors and AI models to deploying the vehicle in real-world environments.

As autonomous vehicle technology continues to evolve, the tools and techniques discussed in this chapter will serve as the building blocks for more advanced systems. With continued advancements in AI, robotics, and sensor technologies, the dream of fully autonomous vehicles is quickly becoming a reality.

Chapter 15: Conclusion: The Road Ahead for AI and Autonomous Vehicles

Introduction: Navigating the Future of Autonomous Vehicles

Autonomous vehicles (AVs) represent one of the most transformative innovations in transportation, offering the potential to reshape how we move, how cities are built, and how economies function. Powered by artificial intelligence (AI), AVs are poised to revolutionize industries, improve road safety, reduce traffic congestion, and enhance efficiency across transportation networks. Yet, as with any groundbreaking technology, the path forward is filled with challenges and opportunities, both technical and societal. In this final chapter, we will explore the current state and future outlook of autonomous vehicle technology, identify emerging trends, discuss career opportunities, and conclude with a hands-on project to build a small autonomous vehicle and prepare it for real-world scenarios.

1. The Current State and Future Outlook of Autonomous Vehicle Technology

The development of autonomous vehicle technology has made incredible progress over the past decade, moving from research labs and prototypes to real-world testing on public roads. Several key milestones have been achieved, but significant hurdles remain before autonomous vehicles can be fully integrated into mainstream society.

1.1 Current State of Autonomous Vehicles

At present, the deployment of autonomous vehicles can be broadly categorized into levels based on the **SAE International's levels of driving automation**:

- **Level 0:** No automation; human drivers are in full control.

- **Level 1:** Driver Assistance; features like adaptive cruise control or lane-keeping assist are available.

- **Level 2:** Partial Automation; the vehicle can control steering and acceleration, but the driver must remain engaged.

- **Level 3:** Conditional Automation; the vehicle can handle all driving tasks in certain conditions, but a human driver must be ready to take over if necessary.

- **Level 4:** High Automation; the vehicle can handle all driving tasks within specific operational conditions (such as within a geofenced area) without human intervention.

- **Level 5:** Full Automation; no human intervention is required at all, and the vehicle can operate in any environment.

Currently, many AVs on the road are at **Level 2** or **Level 3**, with some companies like Waymo and Tesla advancing towards Level 4. For example, **Waymo** has been conducting successful tests of its **Level 4 autonomous taxis** in limited geofenced areas, while **Tesla** has introduced its **Full Self-Driving (FSD)** feature, although it still requires human oversight.

1.2 Key Technologies Driving AV Development

The current success of AV technology relies on several key technologies working together. These include:

- **Artificial Intelligence (AI) and Machine Learning:**
  AI algorithms process vast amounts of sensor data in real-time to make driving decisions. Deep learning techniques, particularly convolutional neural networks (CNNs), are used for image recognition, while reinforcement learning allows AVs to continually improve their decision-making abilities through simulated and real-world experiences.

- **Sensors and Perception Systems:**
  AVs rely on a variety of sensors, including lidar, radar, cameras, and ultrasonic sensors, to perceive their environment. These sensors work together to create a **360-degree view** of the surroundings, detect obstacles, recognize traffic signs, and read road markings.

- **Sensor Fusion and Path Planning:**
  Sensor fusion is the process of combining data from multiple sensors to provide a more comprehensive and accurate understanding of the environment. Path planning algorithms then use this data to decide the best route for the vehicle to follow, considering obstacles, traffic conditions, and other dynamic factors.

- **Connectivity and V2X (Vehicle-to-Everything):**
  The future of AVs includes seamless integration with **smart cities** and infrastructure through **Vehicle-to-Everything (V2X)** communication. This allows AVs to communicate with other vehicles, traffic lights, and even pedestrians to optimize traffic flow, prevent accidents, and improve overall system efficiency.

1.3 Future Outlook: Road to Full Autonomy

The journey towards fully autonomous vehicles is well underway, but there are several technological, regulatory, and societal hurdles to overcome before Level 5 autonomy becomes a reality.

- **Technological Challenges:**
  Although significant progress has been made, achieving **reliable perception** and **decision-making** under all real-world conditions remains a major challenge. AVs need to be able to handle complex urban environments, extreme weather, and edge cases that were not adequately covered in training data.

- **Regulatory and Legal Hurdles:**
  Governments around the world are still working to establish consistent regulations for the testing, deployment, and insurance of AVs. There are also unresolved questions about liability in the event of accidents, data privacy, and cybersecurity.

- **Public Trust and Safety Concerns:**
  One of the biggest challenges for AVs is gaining the **trust** of the public. High-profile accidents, such as the fatal Uber self-driving car incident

in 2018, have raised concerns about the safety of autonomous systems. Building trust requires transparent testing, safety standards, and ongoing improvements in AI systems.

- **Infrastructure Adaptation:**
  For AVs to reach their full potential, cities need to modernize infrastructure, including roads, traffic lights, and pedestrian systems, to accommodate autonomous vehicles. Smart cities equipped with sensors, 5G networks, and V2X communication are essential for enabling AVs to function seamlessly in urban environments.

---

2. Emerging Trends: Electric Vehicles, AI-Powered Transportation Systems, and Integration with Other Technologies

The future of transportation is closely tied to several emerging trends, including the rise of electric vehicles (EVs), the integration of AI across all aspects of mobility, and the convergence of AVs with other innovative technologies such as **5G** and **smart cities**.

2.1 Electric Vehicles (EVs) and Autonomous Vehicles

Electric vehicles and autonomous vehicles are converging as two major trends in the automotive industry. The **transition to EVs** is driven by the need to reduce carbon emissions and tackle climate change, while **autonomous driving** aims to enhance safety, reduce congestion, and optimize mobility.

- **The Symbiotic Relationship:**
  Many AV companies, such as **Tesla**, are integrating autonomous technology with electric vehicles, creating a powerful combination that promises to reduce emissions while improving safety and convenience. Electric vehicles are often more suitable for autonomous systems due to their simpler drivetrains and fewer moving parts, making them ideal candidates for AV conversion.

- **Sustainability in AV Development:**
  As the world moves towards sustainability, the adoption of EVs in conjunction with AV technology will be a game-changer. Autonomous electric shuttles, for example, could become the backbone of **shared**

mobility, reducing individual car ownership and further decreasing emissions from urban areas.

2.2 AI-Powered Transportation Systems: MaaS and V2X Integration

Artificial intelligence plays a crucial role in transforming traditional transportation systems into **AI-powered ecosystems**. This is evident in the rise of **Mobility as a Service (MaaS)**, where AI-powered platforms integrate various modes of transportation— such as buses, trains, and AVs—into a single, seamless service.

- **AI in Traffic Management:**
  AI algorithms are being used to optimize traffic flow in real-time, dynamically adjusting signals, and rerouting vehicles to avoid congestion. By collecting and analyzing data from vehicles, sensors, and infrastructure, AI systems can predict traffic patterns, improve public transportation, and enhance the overall efficiency of cities.

- **Vehicle-to-Everything (V2X) and Smart Cities:**
  V2X communication allows AVs to communicate with infrastructure, other vehicles, and pedestrians, enabling

coordinated movement and smarter traffic management. Cities that adopt V2X technology will see significant improvements in road safety, traffic flow, and energy efficiency, as AVs are integrated into the urban ecosystem.

2.3 Integration with Other Technologies: 5G and IoT

The integration of AVs with **5G networks** and the **Internet of Things (IoT)** will unlock even more potential. 5G offers low-latency, high-speed connectivity, essential for real-time communication between AVs, infrastructure, and other devices.

- **IoT in AVs:**
  IoT sensors embedded in vehicles, roads, and traffic systems can provide a constant stream of data to AVs, improving decision-making and safety. For example, IoT-enabled roads could monitor conditions like road surface quality, weather, and traffic, providing real-time data to AVs to help them navigate more efficiently.

3. Career Paths and Opportunities in AI and Autonomous Vehicle Fields

As autonomous vehicle technology continues to develop, there are a wealth of career opportunities in AI, robotics, and autonomous systems. The industry is expanding rapidly, with demand for skilled professionals across various domains.

3.1 AI and Machine Learning Engineer

AI and machine learning engineers are at the core of autonomous vehicle development. These professionals are responsible for creating and refining the algorithms that power AV decision-making, including perception, path planning, and obstacle avoidance.

- **Skills Required:**
  Expertise in deep learning, reinforcement learning, computer vision, and sensor fusion is essential. Proficiency in programming languages such as Python, C++, and ROS is also necessary.

3.2 Robotics Engineer

Robotics engineers design the physical systems that make AVs capable of navigating the world. This includes developing sensors, actuators, and the control systems that drive the vehicle's movements.

- **Skills Required:**
  Experience in robotics, control systems, sensor integration, and hardware-software interfacing is critical. Familiarity with tools like Gazebo and MATLAB can be advantageous.

3.3 Cybersecurity Specialist

As AVs become more connected, cybersecurity specialists will be needed to protect these vehicles from cyberattacks. Ensuring the integrity of software, securing communication systems, and protecting sensitive data will be key to maintaining safety in autonomous systems.

- **Skills Required:**
  Expertise in network security, cryptography, ethical hacking, and real-time security protocols is necessary. Knowledge of ROS security protocols and vehicle-to-everything (V2X) communication security is a plus.

3.4 Urban Planner and Smart City Developer

As AVs are integrated into smart cities, urban planners and smart city developers will be responsible for designing the infrastructure needed to support these vehicles. This includes traffic management systems, V2X communication infrastructure, and EV charging networks.

- **Skills Required:**
  Experience in urban planning, IoT integration, traffic management, and infrastructure design is essential. Familiarity with AI and autonomous vehicle requirements will be increasingly important in shaping the future of smart cities.

3.5 Researcher in Autonomous Systems

The field of autonomous vehicle research is rapidly evolving, with many opportunities for those interested in advancing AV technology. Researchers work on improving algorithms, sensor technology, and overall system performance to move the industry closer to full autonomy.

- **Skills Required:**
  Advanced degrees in AI, robotics, or computer science, along with a deep understanding of AV-related technologies, are typically required.

4. Final Project: Building a Small Autonomous Vehicle and Preparing It for Real-World Scenarios

In this final section, we will walk through the steps to build a small autonomous vehicle. This project will help you apply the concepts and skills you have learned throughout the chapter and prepare the vehicle for real-world testing.

4.1 Choosing the Right Platform

For this project, we will use a **small robot car platform** equipped with basic sensors, including a camera, lidar, and ultrasonic sensors. Platforms such as the **Donkey Car** or **Jetson Nano** can be used for this project, providing a cost-effective and accessible way to start building your own autonomous vehicle.

4.2 Setting Up the Hardware

- **Installing Sensors:**
  Set up the cameras, lidar, and ultrasonic sensors on the robot. Use a Raspberry Pi or Jetson Nano to process data from these sensors.

- **Motor Control:**
  Connect the motor controller to the robot and

configure it for remote control and autonomous operation. We will use ROS to control the motors based on the sensor inputs.

4.3 Writing the AI Models

For this project, we will develop basic AI models for obstacle detection, path planning, and motion control. These models will use sensor data to detect objects, avoid collisions, and navigate to a target.

- **Obstacle Detection:**
  Train a simple object detection model using deep learning algorithms like CNNs to detect obstacles in the robot's path.

- **Path Planning:**
  Use the A* algorithm to plan the vehicle's path from the starting point to the destination while avoiding obstacles.

4.4 Testing and Iteration

Test the vehicle in a controlled environment, such as a lab or parking lot, to evaluate its performance. Make adjustments based on the feedback, improving sensor calibration, path planning, and decision-making algorithms.

Conclusion

The road ahead for AI and autonomous vehicles is filled with immense potential and challenges. While we are still in the early stages of fully autonomous transportation, the progress made so far is paving the way for a safer, more efficient, and sustainable future. As the technology continues to evolve, new opportunities will arise in fields such as AI, robotics, cybersecurity, and smart cities. By building small autonomous vehicles and exploring the underlying technologies, we can contribute to the development of this exciting and transformative industry.

This chapter has covered the current state and future outlook of AVs, emerging trends, career opportunities, and provided a hands-on project to build your own small autonomous vehicle. The future of autonomous mobility is just beginning, and those who engage with the technology today will be at the forefront of tomorrow's transportation revolution.

Printed in Great Britain
by Amazon